INNER SANCTUM EXPOSED

WRITTEN BY

CHRISTOPHER ROMANO

Inner Sanctum

"A private or secret place to which few other people are admitted."

To most, an Inner Sanctum is compared to something physical like Area 51, a testing ground for weapons of destruction, a place we hear about and often question its existence. However, what if it were associated with an environment like your mind? A mental state that few can understand except those who house those emotions, choosing to keep these feelings to themselves.

The two have similar convictions in creating defense mechanisms and influencing judgment on how we perceive our lives and the thoughts, ideas, and use for them having a major influence and impact on the outcome.

The fact that we are all human may be true, but we also need to account for the internal and external stressors in our daily life that contribute to how we function. In your reading, you will see both played a role in my perception of my place in the world. When coping with a chronic condition, the emotional piece to the disease can often be overshadowed by the physical and un-intentionally ignored, where medical intervention may be an option to consider. With the many challenges, a chronic illness often challenges self-awareness and management of psychological and social pieces.

The chapters of this book are chronological and depict a sampling of episodes experienced in my life.

Each chapter has a brief snapshot reflecting on the positive and negative. The consecutive chapters will not pick up where the other left off purposely, leaving the reader wondering what happened next. How would you react if placed in a similar situation? Would you make the necessary changes and move forward? Or let fate take control in dictating the outcome? The answer or choice may come easy, but would those decisions be as easy when influenced by a mental imbalance?

This tell-all memoir surpasses one dimension and reads as autobiographic, poetic, self-motivational, self-awareness, comedic, dramatic, nonfiction, and more. Diabetes, Cancer, and MS, to name a few, are all debilitating diseases where the physical breakdown of the individual becomes apparent to our peers. Inner Sanctum reveals what can transpire in the emotional piece when surviving a severe medical condition and the impact placed on the judgment and thought process.

I am aware this book will be interpreted differently by many; some may be positive, others negative, and some may laugh, cry, or even mock, but ultimately if my message gets out to the many who have experienced similar confrontations with mind over matter and chosen to create an inner sanctum, then my goal has been achieved and this book a success. Welcome to my world.

DEDICATION

Diabetes has created many life lessons, some taking longer to learn than others. When I finally was able to comprehend that I was not only hurting myself and I was also hurting the loved ones around me, my parents, my brother & sister-in-law, my wife at the time, and eventually my two children, I realized they were suffering too. This book would have an eye-opening effect on what I was going through and getting into a battle with my family by my side. Like David versus Goliath, we conquered diabetes. We, versus the situations created by the complications of this disease, were able to work together to get through these perilous times. I love them because they gave me the support, encouragement, and love necessary to survive, not only as an individual but as a family.

"At some point, you will realize that you have done too much for someone, that the only next possible step to do is to stop, Leave them alone. Walk away. It's not like you're giving up, and it's not like you shouldn't try. It's just that you have to draw the line of determination from desperation. What is truly yours will eventually be yours, and what is not, no matter how hard you try, will never be." – Unknown.

Thank you for not stopping or walking away. Christopher

ACKNOWLEDGMENT

My children have often seen the worst of me. They know nothing other than that he was sick or is sick. I cannot go back or look back on the past. I can only look forward to the future but only be optimistic about how many promises they have for their productivity, success, and a great life for the two, but I am here. I am alive; they are my children, and I need to spend time with them. They are my blood; I need to live for them and show them everything I can do for them. I often feel the need to apologize and sit down with my children. Explain to them I'm sorry Daddy did this. Still, I had to also realize I did not create this disease, but I did react to it incorrectly. Despite my conditions, I never missed one day out of their life, Weather it was a ball game, a recital, something at school, or something outside of school, providing transportation to them and friends to get somewhere like the movies or a game at the school. I did my best to be part of their life. I know my kids greatly appreciate everything I've done, but still, to this day, I feel a little guilty that I probably could've given more along the way, but there were many obstacles I could not avoid. I will always realize that my children are always there for me through thick and thin, so I have to be there for them. I signed a contract to be a father, and that contract never ends, being there for both my children, Jordan and Julianna. I will always be there for you, whether here on earth or above; in whatever capacity, I will always be looking out for your best. I will be your protector, your guardian angel. I now realize I have to live for today and everything that comes along with it, Jordan and

Julianna, I can only say I love you and thank you for allowing me the opportunity to not only be your father but inspiring me to pull through and now allowing me to continue to grow with you.

"There isn't time, so brief is life. For the bickering, apologies. Heart burning, calling to account. There is only time for loving. And but an instant, so to speak, for that."- Mark Twain

TABLE OF CONTENTS

INTRODUCTION POEM

'As the day nears the end, I prepare again, I try, but there is no rest for this soul. The nightly ritual, pacing back and forth, the progression of the clock, the passing of time, another day in my life, my little world. Sheltered since a child, yet allowed to mature, my life is frozen, a victim yet blessed in being chosen. For I am not scared and enter the challenge both debilitating yet rewarding. This obstacle is immense, filled with mental emotion as well as physical devotion. I need to reflect, avoid the many mistakes, turn the table and offer a trade. I have taken the punches and endured the drilling; it is time to preach, practice and pay forward what I owe to those eager and willing. To provide but also educate and sympathize by and through my own experiences, providing for the well-being and preserving the bond to which their loved ones will respond. The outgoing support, the respect and the love, a connection of family and God above. I truly believe I was sent with a reason, regardless of the year or the season. Like April showers to represent the tears, the swirling winds of the lion left, and the air I breathe onto others grieving. So, I am here and real, a force to be reckoned with. In this journey, I must also remember that, much like many, I am human, bleed, and cry. I hold onto emotion; our faults and strengths are both bottled up in internal chaos looking to be set free. I had been told when younger that there was a cure that would be, for now, control the disease and don't let it control thee. Using this same philosophy, will there be a cure, or should I say, special someone? Will I be in control, or will fate take over? Not being a man of the cloth and not having much hope, I now kneel and pray to God, the Father, and the Holy Ghost. The years go fast my life might pass; what am I to do? I can't give up because I have two; I signed a contract to get them through. I need to be strong and provide to give up on them would be suicide. A second chance has come; my prayers were met; February, she came an Angel was sent. You see, I am not looking for an answer, instead inviting the one who holds the key, with the slightest turn completing me....'

CHAPTER 1: GAME DAY, OR SO I THOUGHT?

"It's a beautiful day for a ballgame." - Ernie Banks, Baseball HOF.

The day couldn't have started any better--well, at least for a 14-year-old and his start to spring. I quickly glanced out my bedroom window: the sun shined bright, and the window was cracked just enough to feel a cool breeze and whiff of the fresh-cut grass.

It was going to be a good day. I was eager to get up and get over to the baseball diamond; today was not only our first game, but we would also be getting our brand-new uniforms in which, ironically, I always chose the #13--but was it really lucky? Things may prove different this year, but I was wearing it regardless. It was just a matter of time before I could strap on my cleats, slide on my glove, and get ready to toss that first pitch. Just a quick visit for my annual physical with Dr. B, and I was good to go. Mom and I got in the car and made our way to the office, which was only a 15-minute ride, and she could see the excitement in my eyes and hear it in the tone of my voice that this appointment couldn't be over any quicker, so I could get to my safe place. Anything dealing with a sport I played was like a comfort zone and allowed me to excel at something I was good at. It also provided a sense of security over the fact I was somewhat overweight--one of my insecurities. But with sports, it was different: I was good, maybe one of the best at my age in the leagues I played, and I wasn't looked at by my peers as an overweight kid; I was looked at like an athlete with potential. We spent quite some time in Dr. B's office, and I was getting anxious. "What the hell is going on?" and "Where did my mother disappear to?" I thought.

One last glance at the clock, and I realized I was already running late in making it to the field and found myself pacing back and forth; and then they appeared, not only Dr. B but Mom. They were bouncing information off each other as if it were a Q&A session on how to fix a flat or take part in a new procedure; ironically, that was just what it was.

'Off we went; we waited in a room, eyes on the clock. The warm-ups would start soon. Where was the doctor? Why so long, getting anxious, feeling like a never-ending song? Into the room would enter the doctor; with a few quick words, there would be no soccer. My response would be innocent and a bit uncertain, "Doc, I have time to wrap this up., I'll be fine. The room grew cold, and the emotion grew grim; not today, son, you're checking in....'

So, what the hell does one pack for a hospital stay, and just how long would I be there?

When I leave, will I be cured? I had so many things racing through my mind, but at 14, my only concern was missing opening day at the little league field. Really, I should have been asking myself why I was so sick and didn't even know it. Mom grabbed a duffle bag and threw everything imaginable in it, from clean undies to comic books; at that point, I knew the stay was more than just an overnight sleepover. Can't say that I was nervous, maybe more confused, but the facial expressions made by Mom and the watery eyes all led me to believe none of this was good. Amidst all this, my father, who held a full-time job selling insurance, was thrown into a whirlwind of information: First off, what the hell is my son going through? Secondly, how is my wife, his mother, handling this, and what were all these new gadgets and prescriptions he needed to buy and fill so his son could survive and function in this world of medical mishaps?

After a 4-day stint in the local hospital, I was given my walking papers; the physicians and medical staff decided the family was prepared to do battle and could start a vigorous lifestyle with the inclusion of Type I Diabetes. Everything would be revised in my daily life, and the change also created a major commitment from my family. As a kid, yes, insulin injections, watching what I ate, and constantly monitoring my blood sugar became a way of life; but it also felt like losing it!!

The teen years were definitely the toughest. Going from a pre-pubescent child to a maturing adult. Not only was I changing physically but mentally as well. Life was better managed at this time, seeing I had mom as a caretaker, figuring out my insulin and meals, and a large enough group of friends who had accepted the disease I had and would always arrange things around it, so I felt like the normal kid I was. But again, I felt like I was living two separate lives.

During this phase, we did experience quite a few scares: low blood sugar, high blood sugar, my mental outbursts because I thought I was "broken," and a slow separation from my current endocrinologist, whom I felt was just too controlling for my personality, regardless of her looking out for my best health.

"There must be two of me: the 'I' and the 'self.'" - Eckhart Tolle

CHAPTER 2: SKILLS CHALLENGE

I found such solace in the feel of the cold air that came off the cold ice during hockey season and the smell of fresh-cut grass on the baseball diamond; I craved sports all year round. This was my comfort zone, a second home where I could excel and show what I could do. And for that one to two hour, I could feel free, independent, and untouchable; I was a good athlete and noticed for it.

I received awards, and I got acknowledgments from different schools, sometimes even a college; these awards graced my walls; my work ethic in these areas was demanding and challenging, but I put in the time, and it all paid off when it was time to perform. Needless to say, the same did not go for my diabetes. Coaches were thrilled to have me as part of their team. They often asked if I brought my go-go juice--when they referred to go-go juice, they meant my Gatorade, my OJ, my little burst of life that kept my sugars running; little did they know it wasn't just giving me that needed burst but escalating my sugars extremely high past the norm.

Although it was an extremely dangerous boost, I often felt it gave me superhuman powers: the ability to skate faster, throw harder, hit farther, and endure that hour to two hours on the field or ice. Needless to say, my concern on the day or night of a game was to compete and win when I was actually losing part of my life. All my focus on game day was just that: the ability to play and not on school, or moreover, not on my diabetes and the game of survival.

When coming down from that sugar high, the feelings weren't as pleasant, as you felt the fatigue, the tiredness, the soreness, wanting to just roll over and take a nap or sit for a moment to regain your breath, but at the time, all well worth it. On the day of a game or on the eve of practice, all my focus was on either a hockey puck or baseball.

That was all that mattered. Nothing else was my concern. This was my chance to escape for a while, that moment where I could be made a "perfect me" Nothing else existed except scoring goals or rounding bases. I was determined to become that top athlete; little did I know how much ignorance would play a role in my physical and mental deterioration. Slowly but surely, the utilization of the so-called go-go juice, intending to raise my blood sugars to perform, started to take its toll. My muscles grew weak. They were also cramped. My strength was dwindling, my skills were lacking. I could no longer skate around a player with no effort, nor could I hit a ball as far as it was meant to go.

I can remember a teammate once asking me in the locker room how long I had been diabetic, which at the time was around 3 to 4 years; he followed by replying that his brother was diabetic, and as he got older, he also became impotent. At first, I thought he said important, and I thought, wow, what was he considered before important to him in his life? Then it registered he meant impotent. (Let's just say at 17, I was educated enough by the Sex Ed teacher in high school, Mrs. K, to know what this traumatizing occurrence or loss to manhood meant, i.e., "limp dick, wet noodle'"... yeah, you get the point. This topic will be revisited as we get deeper into the book.)

The ice felt like skating in quicksand, and rounding third base felt like I was being chased and running for my life; I was out of breath, struggling to get home. I would do this for approximately four years, basically the whole time I was in high school; I utilized this method as what I thought was an advantage when it was really my downfall; behind the scenes, these escalated blood sugars were slowly creating damage to all the nerves which ran throughout my body, better known as neuropathy.

I also began to take on a different appearance. I began to lose weight rapidly. I'm talking pounds per day. I was in keto-acidosis; with keto-acidosis, my body was not utilizing the proteins I was taking in as they were meant to be used. I urinated like a fountain out of control, releasing whatever proteins were consumed earlier that day as liquid waste.

On the other hand, this was great: I was a bit on the heavy side, and any weight loss to me was welcome in my appearance and possibly added attraction from the female following despite not being quite the ladies' man. Although happy with the change in appearance, my focus was still not on girls but on sports, my escape, and my safe place. It wasn't 'til the last game of my senior year, when I was part of quite a vicious hit from an opposing player on the ice--I went down and slowly got up--that I noticed something was not right.

Usually, I would spring to my feet, but not this time. I literally crawled off that ice that night. I made my way to the locker room, and with some assistance, even removing my skates, I sat in tears. I knew it was time. This was over, the damage was done, but the damage created was much worse because my diabetes was out of control. I often second-guessed: if I were in control, would I have performed at the top level If I were in control of my diabetes, would these injuries be less of a factor? But the bottom line is today, I sit with pieces of paper showing all the goals I achieved, all the acknowledgments I gained, and reflect on all the measures I took to get there... yet I never played hockey or baseball again. I'm not in the NHL or the MLB, but I do sit here today with a tremendous amount of diabetic neuropathy and many of the complications it presented, the unwanted trophies.

At this time, my mind was still not wholly sound, not realizing the risk and only the rewards. There comes a time when you've been out of control for so long that your muscles begin to atrophy; what I mean by this is they die, no longer grow, and no longer function the way they were meant to be used. As a result, I was a patient of occupational and physical therapy, all done within the local hospital. Not only was I not eager to be a participant in this exercise regimen, but I also was not in favor of a return to a Medical environment, the opposite of my safe place, the place I often cringed to think of, somewhere, I considered far from home. Much like steroids or enhancing drugs, in my case, that go-go juice, sometimes the reward is not always worth the risk, and my main reason for sticking this chapter within the pages of this book. I struggled with this lesson for quite some time because I always wanted to be at the top of my game. I often didn't think of the consequence. I would push that back behind, bury it deep and choose to move forward, taking risks to be what I thought was my best at that time. OT and PT went on for months and never quite got me back to where my performance used to be. It was a definite aid and a start, far from where I needed to be. The point being made, at one point, awards, certificates coach recognition all surrounded me and gave me self-awareness, and I was somebody, somebody people had looked at as productive, unique, and stood out above the rest. I may still have those pieces of paper or awards made of tin, but the only thing I gained came as a loss, and it's the neuropathy I suffer today.

"You want to remain hungry and stay in a good place as a competitor; simultaneously, you want to be confident, not cocky. You must realize that you can lose. We must stay hungry because losing is the worst thing to happen now. That's a road we don't want to go down. - Lamar Odom Athlete/Author)

CHAPTER 3: LET IT RIDE

Life is filled with many temptations and depending on your willpower, we often find ourselves catering to the opportunity. Some good, some bad, but ultimately, we become embraced by that situation. Privileged with a junior driver's license and a blue Pontiac at my disposal, I now broadened my ability to see the world. In my case, the Friday nightlife with the rest of the dreamers at Yonkers Raceway. You came here to take the risk of padding your bank account or busting your wad and leaving you even more depressed than when you entered the door to the building. Living at home and having a job at the local deli paid just enough to put gas in the tank and provide for this special occasion.

So here was my opportunity to take the money and double, triple, or regretfully piss it down the drain. With me, it was always the reward outweighing the risk, and again, my mind was focused on the pot of gold at the end of the rainbow and not the leprechaun preventing me from doing so or what it would take to get there.

I was so focused on dropping that first bet on the ponies that it didn't even register I was still 16 years old. But I was determined to pass my wager by the veteran who sat behind the window taking my offer and the rest of the regulars who occupied space at this establishment.

Much like life gambling for me was a fifty/fifty chance. You either win, or you lose. You either chose to live or to die. One way or the other, by the end of the night, the day, the week, the year, you knew your fate. If that sounds familiar, you are right. Similar to gambling, I approached my life with diabetes and its control the same way.

Willing to take the risk on a jockey and the horse he rode in on, I placed my bet. Convinced the races weren't fixed and willing to accept the reputation for it, I would bet safe but large. I would always bet the favorite knowing two things: the chances of winning were most probably a given, and two, the odds would not allow for a big payday. Problem solved; drop a "bomb" on the favorite. When I say bomb, I mean whatever money lined my pocket when I left my house was now backed by a ticket printed on a piece of paper.

I had some time to debate over my pick, and there were 20 minutes to post, or should I say the start of the race. I needed to kill some time, so let's eat. You wouldn't think so, but eating at the track was actually a bit taxing on my funds. But it didn't matter. I was hungry and had access to all the foods not favorable to the diet of a Type-I diabetic.

I don't think I would call Yonkers Raceway a safe place, but for that 2-3 hour, I felt like I could be myself and in control. I didn't have to worry about my appearance; I was independent and socialized with the many patrons wired the same way I was, carefree up until the shot sounded for the race to begin.

As I stuffed my face with a greasy quarter pounder and fries, washing it down with a 32-ounce Coke (not diet), I would people-watch. Not registering at the time, I was looking at a reflection of myself and who I had become;

Everyone and anything that shows up in our life is a reflection of something that is happening inside of us." –Alan Cohen.

So many familiar faces recognized, people I now knew by first name. The best friends during the time spent at the track, especially if you had a tip on a race or were willing to splurge in buying them a cup of Joe. Needless to say, once you departed from the track, they were just as much a stranger as the guy who took my money, adding to the raceways surplus of losing tickets. But I didn't care; I was in the moment. I fit in with them. They accepted me, and my mind was telling me this is where I belong. Was this the land of opportunity? Making so-called friends, a little bit of money, and dining on unforbidden cuisine.

Ironically, I had quite the knack, or should I say, picking winners and would often leave the track with a pocket full of money. Now accompanied by my attraction to food, I was developing an addiction to gambling.

Before giving in to my new vice, I needed to figure out if I hit big, how could I collect? For the most part, winnings came in the form of hundreds of dollars. What if it were more, thousands? Well, I guess I would soon find out.

That night the cards were in my favor, and I decided to be bold and go with the long shot. A 30-1 risk. I was all in, feeling a little nervous after fronting a $100 stake on this stallion (female horse). Mentally I was only computing what I could possibly walk away with and not the loss of any profit I made.

Before confronting the ticket taker, I needed to make the usual stop. By this time, the food I engorged myself in was about ready to exit the building. I didn't have a weak stomach, but my pancreas was angry, and whatever insulin it was still producing went on strike. Raising my sugars well above 300 mg/dl. I could only guess? Not concerned with testing my blood sugar or taking additional insulin to combat the spike. My body needed to release these unwanted sugars. I went about my business (literally) and raced to get my bet in. With less than 1 minute to post, I sat back, a little drained following the cleanse, and hoped for the best.

Cut to the chase. My horse crossed the finish line with grace. She was not even challenged from the get-go. Her ride is a pleasure to watch and, in this case, be part of.

With the ticket in hand, something clicked. Like a human calculator, I didn't even have to guess. I knew the payout was substantial. How could I collect? Was I willing to approach the teller and possibly be proofed before I received this reward? Should I take that chance and forfeit my earnings if I am deemed underage and betting illegally? Hell no! This was one of the few times I had actually thought about the risk over the reward. My wheels were turning, and the manipulation I possessed went into action. I know. I'll get one of my newfound friends to do it. Flip them a couple of bucks, and they were good. But now we're back to risk? What if this individual takes the money and runs? What if he gets aggressive and threatens me? My mind was so fucked up at this time. I wasn't looking at the big picture of losing out on $3000 but instead seeing it as risking the loss of only what I had started with, which was $100. Worst case scenario, I lose out on money I never really had, I don't get my asked kicked by some vagrant, and I don't get arrested by authorities for underage gambling.

The night played out in my favor, with no handcuffs, no bumps or bruises, and my pockets a little deeper. But despite all that drama, what did I achieve? I didn't feel any happier, the excitement was short-lived, and I was still alone, looking for my next fix to fill my emotional void.

That night I walked away a winner but, at the same time, a loser. Underlying this 2-3 hour release was the boycott of my condition and lack of control over this part of life. My horse won the race crossing the finish line, but I failed to acknowledge the Friday night excursions were adding to my falling to the back of the pack in my own race or, should I say, life.

"If someone is falling behind in life, you don't have to remind them. Believe me, they already know. If someone is unhealthy, they know. If someone is failing at work, they know. If someone is struggling in their relationships, with money, with self-image... they know. It's what consumes their thoughts each day". – Brianna Wiest

The problem was I knew it but wasn't on board with doing anything about it. I did realize there is a similarity between life and gambling, which is risk and reward. But at the same time, I failed to realize they're very different at the same time. With each paycheck came another chance or opportunity. But with life, you're only given one, and once it's taken, there is no getting it back; there is no rebound. The only deposit made is not to the bank, but to your body and soul 6 feet under the soil I once stood.

"An act of thinking without restriction-without boundaries or rules can lead to the point of no return." – Sean William Scott.

CHAPTER 4: THE BOOGEY MAN

It was mid-winter and extremely cold outside. Not that I ventured out much, but most activities were done indoors. No different than any other night, I found myself alone and just trying to keep busy. I had been watching TV for a couple of hours and flipped through a couple of my favorite comics. My mind was in overdrive, and I found it extremely hard to knock off for the night. The bedroom I often considered a safe place, felt more like a cell with padded walls. All I wanted to do was bounce from one to the next until I was so physically exhausted I had no choice but to close my eyes. But this did not happen. Besides, I still had to play out the nightly ritual of taking my meds, making sure not to skip a dose.

After following protocol, I decided to make an effort. Shutting the lights, I made my way to the bed and crawled under the covers. Gradually I started to drift off but, at the same time, fought to stay awake. Did I think I was going to miss something? Finally, I managed to let myself go. I couldn't have passed counting my third sheep before I was woken from this short-lived trance. Something was tugging at my toes? I normally experienced some twitching due to my neuropathy or a small cramp. But this was different. Something was actually making me uncomfortable. I shifted my position in the bed and decided to try this again. No sooner than I closed my eyes, there it was again. Pulling at my sheets. Now frustrated, I got out of bed and turned on the lights. Like a detective, I began to inspect the room. But what the hell was I looking for? Convinced I was the only person occupying the room, and there was no monster living beneath my bed. I made my return.

This time feeling a little paranoid armed with a flashlight in hand. I laid back down, determined to catch this bastard if he tried it again. Sounds crazy, which it probably is, but not at that time.

"What the fuck? Where are you? It happened again. My light illuminated the room, but again, just me and the strong belief I was not alone. Not only was I awake, but so were my parents, who occupied the room down the hall. I heard the footsteps coming closer; it was my father. My focus was not on his voice asking me 'is everything ok" but my attention directed at whatever was invading my safe place. It was as if Dad didn't exist. I would repeat the process of turning off my light source with the intention of exposing the culprit when I turned it back on. Things were only getting worse as I threatened to kick the shit out of the monster inside my head. Seeing he had no success in getting through to me, my father recruited my brother, who had just come home from a night out with friends. Chiming in, "Chris, what's going on?" I had no response for him; only more profanity spewed at the one who kept messing with my sheets. By this time, there was a short silence. Then crack! A bit startled by my delusion, my bedroom door came flying inward. My brother had kicked in the door. Not knowing how to react, I became combative, as if my father, brother, and my unidentified friend were all playing on the same team.

From this point, I grew numb and didn't offer the trade-in conversation. Probably because I didn't know what to say. How can I explain my reaction to something that didn't exist? Can you imagine the response if I answered, "I am just playing peek-a-boo with the boogeyman"? By this point, I was being forcefully restrained by my father, who now pressed upon my chest. Holding me down. I knew I was sickly, but I was still stronger. Part of me was saying push back and remove this man who had now entered my personal space. The other half said this is my father. He's doing what's best. I live under his roof, and these are his rules. My mental state was compromised, and under the influence of a narcotic recently prescribed and obviously not regulated, I felt two quick brushes past my cheek. A wake-up call from my father's open hand. Competent enough to realize the connection between father and son, something registered. As I eased back before any harm was done.

"Your mind will play tricks on you, and your eyes will deceive you. But your heart will tell you the truth." - Anonymous.

Managing to coax Dad into letting me go, the battle would continue on and off through the night. I was out of control, and so was the situation. Sirens could be heard as multiple vehicles, including the town paddy wagon, came to a stop at 53 Lyons Rd. The place I called safe was now in turmoil. The last recollection of this encounter was me being escorted from my bedroom. Making my way down a path lined with officers, most of whom I knew on a first-name basis. There were no cameras or the local news, but that night I did feel like I was on display for the paparazzi. Soon to be accompanied by rumors circulated among the townies.

So where do I find fault in this situation? Who is to blame? Sure, I think there is a strong argument in pointing a finger in the direction of the doctors and the meds prescribed. But once again, I need to re-visit the question commonly asked, "If the diabetes were under control and I respected the condition by adhering to the lifestyle it brought with it, would I be in this position"?

"Smart people learn from their mistakes. But the real sharp ones learn from the mistakes of others". - Brandon Mull

When it comes to the treatment of a disease. In my case, it was Type I-Juvenile Diabetes; the treatment of this chronic illness commonly includes the long-term use of insulin and the possibility of additional pharmaceuticals. Insulin not being a choice but a necessity. Although these medications are effective in controlling the disease, the lack of adherence to a prescribed regimen is often ignored by 50% of the population. Finding myself as guilty.

It is only normal, as with human nature, that most choose not to take medications because they worry about side effects. And some just don't embrace the idea of needing to take any medicine. This was my case.

I do support that diet, exercise, and medication prescribed as needed are crucial in maintaining physical well-being, but when dealing with the mental state of my persona, I have never been an advocate for its inclusion, and with good reason. True, a successful treatment plan is based on trial and error and how you respond to the newly prescribed concoction, but my position is not to become a human guinea pig. Only to realize the negative outweighs the positive. Leaving me with a question?

Are these major pharmaceutical companies just out to gain from your illness or really interested in an attempt to better the way you deal with your life mentally and physically. This topic can be debated for years to come and is outside the scope of my writing. But does create a reason for concern.

"Drugs are reality's legal loopholes." - Jeremy P. Johnson, American Aphorist.

CHAPTER 5: COLLEGE BLUES

I don't want to make the comparison, but leaving home for the first time on my own would be an enormous challenge; much like the pages or scenes in a National Geographic documentary, I was leaving the nest. Although by choice, it was like the momma bird pushing me over the cliff and saying fly. I was entering the so-called institution where I would grow mentally and be ready for what opportunities were available in the real world, or so I thought. I can honestly say college did not provide or prepare me for the outside world, a job, a career, or just a simple way to approach what we call reality. Then again, I cannot say that at this point, I was even living in reality or in real-time, focusing on the future; the monkey was still on my back (diabetes), and I was still perplexed about how to deal with this disease.

"To the youngsters of today, I say belief in the future, the world is getting better, there is still plenty of opportunity." - Walt Disney.

I asked again: am I one person or living two separate lives in my mind? Regardless, not that I accepted it, I was much at fault, not the college and its educators. Not only was I mind-fucking the professors but also myself by not putting in the required attendance, participation, and focus on classes, not being able to process who was really fooling whom. Literally being away from home for a half-semester, my physical and mental capabilities were being severely compromised through the mismanagement of my condition (diabetes); much to my dismay, I could not see, let alone accept this.

"Trying to please everybody is impossible. If you did that, you'd end up in the middle with nobody liking you. You've just got to make the decision you think is your best and do it." - John Lennon.

I knew I was not stable and only getting sicker by the day, but I tried to hide this from my consciousness and everyone around me. What was so odd, not to me but probably noted by others, was that something was wrong with this picture I portrayed, yet I was comfortable with it.

"The more you like yourself, the less you are like anyone else, which makes you unique." - Walt Disney

I even became a master manipulator with my professors, using my illness as an excuse for missing class or project deadlines on the syllabus. However, I was still surviving both college and more importantly, life. There came a certain point where some issues, like frequent urination and vomiting, became unavoidable, but it was happening so often, the norm in my daily routine. I would wake early as if pregnant with morning sickness, vomiting whatever I ingested the night before. In addition, I was still urinating so frequently I probably should have had a catheter inserted to save on the time I spent in a bathroom or risked being caught peeing in a nearby bush and avoiding wetting myself like a newborn in a diaper.

The people who were the closest to me saw that the clothes I wore hung off me. I used to dress meticulously; now, my hygiene was lacking, and if in my vicinity, the sweet smell of nectar permeated from my skin, which wasn't due to B.O.

but rather to elevated blood sugars. I lost twenty-plus pounds after returning home from college. I was so fatigued and unconcerned by my appearance that the sweet nectar I mentioned even went undetected by my senses.

Even though I was eating, and I should say excessively, my body was not assimilating any of its nutrients. The so-called proteins or building blocks we call nourishment were being excreted from my body by spilling over into my urine due to the excessively high blood sugars. Little did I know I was experiencing all the signs of being in keto-acidosis? This metabolic imbalance is a process similar to today's ever-popular KETO diet, which I am still skeptical about if followed long-term. Additionally, seeing my body wasn't getting the required nutrients or hydration, my skin was dry and would flake; when I removed my socks, it was like a fine cloud of powder which was actually dead skin. My nails began to crack easily; if not enough, my hair began to fall out in clumps that couldn't be disguised with the old-school comb over. My body was releasing excessive amounts of urine, to the point I recall one instance when I had just made it home, feeling the urge to pee, ready to burst like a geyser. Quickly, I found myself with the car pulled over and relieved in the middle of the street. Now relieved, something else drew my attention: I failed to put my car in park, and it was slowly rolling backward? Luckily, the car slowly stopped when it rubbed the street curb; no one was hurt, and my car was unscathed, plus I was dry down below.

As I continued to shed body weight by the pounds, I also introduced something new to my dietary regime, allowing me to eat whatever I wanted, no matter the number of calories or, my worst enemy, the sugar content. I'm talking about; you guessed it, a laxative. This little flavorful piece of chocolate acted as a dessert or end to my meals; it tasted good and worked quickly. Little did I know at this time just how much damage I was doing to my body and how it functioned; I was developing a condition called Bulimia. I found the food was comforting and encouraged by having this added weapon to my arsenal, where eating filled a lot of my voids, like friends and interest in school, and I found myself doing nothing because I was cutting classes and had endless time available to me. Much like an aspiring actor getting their fifteen minutes of fame, the twenty or more minutes I allotted to gorge on copious amounts of food and sugary beverages allowed me a brief escape from the world and, more importantly, diabetes. Not only was I coherent, conscious, and well-understood in what I was doing to my body, any complications that I would endure did not register in my mind. Big deal, little diarrhea, vomiting, and frequent urination... all well worth it at the time, and best of all, not a pound of weight registered on the scale. So what if I appeared a bit disheveled in my now oversized clothing? I now had a feeling of being in control over my own daily schedule, independent, yet far from it.

"Despite everything, no one can dictate who you are to others." -Prince

This ceremonious calling would occur every day over the next couple of months. If the fridge were empty, I would call for take-out; if the restaurant were closed, I'd hit the vending machines. Of course, there were times I ran out of money and found myself scrounging for my roommate's scraps and, embarrassingly enough, food strangers left behind. My body became a machine, and I couldn't get enough fuel to keep it going, but I had just enough sugar to contribute to my downward spiral.

"I think it's important to have good hard failures when young. I learned a lot from that. Because it makes you aware of what can happen to you." -Walt Disney

CHAPTER 6: PRACTICE WHAT YOU PREACH

Continuing the conversation on school and work, both having the tendency not to be my favorites at the time, I wanted to address a specific day amongst my fellow students when I felt the need to address the topic of diabetes vicariously. I liked the students to understand that diabetes acted as a double-edged sword in my life; it created complications and obstacles, forced me to mature and grow quicker, and became more alert to what was happening in the world. It forced my body to make adjustments that would accommodate me through life. Dealing with something that was at the time severely out of control, I happened to be a dietetic technician student at Westchester Community College.

We were asked to speak on topics concerning us, those we were either familiar with or needed to research. I thought, what better topic than diabetes? Not only do I know a lot about it, but I live with it; let me see if I can enlighten my peers a little bit on what it's like to live with diabetes--not to make it look like a negative, but also to show them the positives for the diabetic. Create a poster about what they need to know to be in control and how hard it is to remain in power.

I thought I would do something fun, create packages of handouts, different types of supplies utilized by a diabetic, different blood value work-up sheets, the whole kit and caboodle; not only would I be informative, but I would also be demonstrative in the way I presented this topic. In addition to what I had learned through living with this disease, I invested quite some time in putting together a presentation that I'd be familiar with and comfortable getting up before my peers. At first, I was a bit nervous as I went to the front of the room that day, but it seemed like second nature once I got going. I had done this before. I explained to the students how I could categorize it: living with diabetes. You used the word 'life' because that's exactly what it was. You had a lifestyle you were living with; you had to deal with it, cope with it, and hopefully make the best of it to have the best life you could possibly have, despite this debilitating disease. Life is not only a word; but represents something. So I broke down each letter into a category that exemplified what we, as diabetics, go through daily.

As I said, I wanted my colleagues at the time to come away from this lecture not with a negative but with a positive as well. I want to be able to show that, yes, there are negative effects to the disease; but if controlled properly, there can also be positive things in life. The individual can completely control the disease.

I begin with the letter L in life.

I stated that L can stand for two different things: losing or learning. Looking at the negative, in terms of losing (if diabetes were to go uncontrolled) ... obviously, you would lose the battle. Still, if you took the time to learn, you would educate yourself on how to make the necessary adjustments to control your blood sugars, make the right food choices, make the right medical or medication changes, and have your sugars in complete check.

Moving onto the letter I explained, it could also be used for ignorance, meaning you were in denial. You refused to believe you had this disease and left it untreated. On the other hand, we could look at it as insulin. Insulin is like the wonder drug, allowing you to eat and control your blood sugars, preventing any complications. Due to being under tight control, F could stand for 'failure again' if we choose not to treat our symptoms or recognize that we are living with a disease. It ultimately would lead to failure, but if we pay attention to these symptoms, we could lead quite a normal life.

The symptoms that I was trying to explain, or the experience of low and high blood sugars, that erratic roller coaster ride of the highs and lows... most of this revolves around food, the F in life. By creating food logs and adjusting our insulin properly, we could learn, make the proper insulin adjustments, and avoid any of these typical situations where the rollercoaster rides would end. With slight tweaks to medication, we would find most foods practical for diabetes, even if you wanted that ice cream sundae or cupcake.

The last component of the word 'life' begins with the letter E. Some people can take that E as standing for 'exit' or "I need to get the hell away from this disease." I do feel that way as well, but it's something you need to face; it's something you're born with or inherit or develop later in life, and you need to address it head-on. The area I am speaking of is exercise. Usually, when you exercise, your body utilizes whatever food has been put into your body to decrease your blood sugars. Decrease them to a point where we can function properly, but we also must be aware not to have them drop too quickly or too low. Creating a low blood sugar again would fall under the category of 'learning,' so you see when you utilize all four letters in the word' life,' you can quite easily learn to maintain control of your diabetes, giving yourself a better percentage rate at avoiding future complications.

Leaving the lecture hall that day, I felt quite good about what I had illustrated. I thought I gave some guidance, education, and probability. I also felt that I provided promise. It's quite true to say that diabetes can be seen as a debilitating issue, but it can also be seen as a positive if handled the right way. At the end of the commencement, I was approached by many students, and I encouraged them to ask questions. I felt confident in the answers I'd be able to provide; not only was it rewarding to see the interest that had been generated by students, but the compliments I received from my instructor at the time also provided a sense of accomplishment in what I had set out and plan to do I had accomplished. Hopefully, I gave those students a different impression or outlook on how people live and deal with diabetes.

The only negative I took away from me that particular day was that I was really lying to myself. I spit out all this information on how to adopt a positive lifestyle and keep your diabetes in check; however, I was not living that way. I did not practice what I preach; truthfully, I was well aware of this and realized I was the only one at fault, who made no real aggressive attempt by living by those 4 letters in LIFE, and my complications would only further progress.

"The meaning of life is not to simply exist to survive; it's to move ahead, to go up, to achieve, and to conquer."- Arnold Schwarzenegger.

On that day, I walked out of the classroom, relieved of the pressures of the presentation. But was I really practicing what I preached? Or was I still utilizing the art of manipulation, which I had down to a science and used before with professors, doctors, and my own family? These were young students out to learn and sponges soaking up information to be used in the field they were studying, most of whom were my friends or classmates. Was I truly in this position at the time to educate another, or was I merely out there for me and an A in the class I seldom attended? I can honestly say probably a little of both.

"For a moment, he felt good about this. A moment or two later, he felt bad about feeling good about it." - Douglas Adams (Author)

CHAPTER 7: DOCTOR G.

On one of my many hospital stays, I found myself, as usual, under constant observation by doctors and nurses. Not only were these medical liaisons keeping an eye on my physical health, like blood and urine (as well as my conditioning), I noticed other doctors of a different sort appearing. One day a dietician, another a psychologist or psychiatrist... so my curiosity and wheels began to spin: why were they here? What do they see? Moreover, what did they want? Seeing no progress was made to recover to what was considered healthy. Apparently, doctors felt the other piece to the puzzle not being addressed was my state of mind:

'Many people in this world or that walk this earth will never understand what it's like to live with a disease or hear the voices people talk about unless you are going through it yourself. They will also ask why? He was so young, or he had so much to give. But they can't understand: you cannot give when another something is constantly taking.' Anonymous

At this point, I had already been in the hospital for over a month and felt like a human guinea pig, where any testing or procedure a doctor thought might benefit my health was performed. I constantly found myself being hooked up to an IV and having blood drawn every hour on the hour; so yes, between sleep deprivation, dehydration, and the different cocktails of medications being taken, I was like a zombie, most often, and as a minor un-able to resist their demands, that meant remaining in the hospital.

Days became cyclic, knowing when a nurse would show, a meal would be, and even when my roommate had to go sit upon his throne. I thought to myself: how much more of this can I take? Will I ever see the comfort of my own home again? Will I ever just open the fridge door to get something to eat? And more importantly, when would I regain my independence to come and go as I please, without a set of eyes on me? Strangely enough, this would not happen any time soon. I remember asking my mother why the doctors and staff were handling my situation the way they were; I wanted answers and had passed my patience threshold. At times I even found myself disgruntled with a nurse, second-guessing a doctor, and spewing profanity.

That night, in somewhat of a need in the way of a mood adjustment, I asked my mother flat-out, "You see what this shit is?" At that time, I was pointing out something written on my dinner menu card and holding up a plastic fork. It said: "'Patient to only utilize plastic cutlery.'

Well, Mom had an answer for me. She said that in one of my shit fits, I threatened to jump out the window, so I was considered at high risk of harming myself. Although not funny, considering the hospital windows only opened far enough to slide a piece of paper through, I still threatened to do so. Inevitably I was just starting to lose it mentally, and the decline was happening quickly. At this point, Mom was pretty much a built-in roommate from the early hours until the sun went down; it also became her second home, and little did I realize what type of stress she was going through. She was strong and motivating and did whatever she needed to pull me through.

At times I found myself even getting short with my mom; all she wanted was for her son to come home healthy, maintaining and enjoying life through the eyes of a child. She wanted to give me back my innocence, my will, and my freedom to breathe the air once again. I, on the other hand, was losing the will:

"Stop trying to control everything and just let go. Let go!" - Tyler Durden (Fight Club)

At this point, not only had days passed, but the visit started turning into weeks and months. I was still a patient at the same hospital, undergoing all the same services. Why wouldn't I find my way back on track? Why couldn't these doctors pinpoint how to get me under control? Most days consisted of getting out of bed to walk and stretching; afterward, it would be a free-for-all. Maybe read, maybe watch TV, and of course, those in-between meals that came like clockwork and the ever-so-familiar face of a nurse telling me, "It's time for your vitals."

Vitals meant sticking your finger, testing your blood sugar, taking your insulin... all the things I despised and alienated me from being the normal person I wanted to be. I felt broken and damaged. Why couldn't I just eat a meal when I wanted? Why couldn't I just walk out the door when I wanted? What was going on? Nobody knew, and if they did, they weren't telling me.

That evening my schedule was changed a bit. One of my favorite songs by the Scorpions, "Send Me an Angel," might as well have been playing:

"The wise man said just raise your hand and reach out for the spell/Find the door to the Promised Land/ just believe in yourself/ hear this voice from deep inside/it's the call of your heart /Close your eyes, and you will find the way out of the dark."

She had long, pulled-back blonde hair, the complexion of an angel, all dressed in white, and wore high heels. My schedule changed slightly that evening when I knew her face had appeared. Who was she? Was she here to see me?

I had never seen her before, but she came in and addressed herself as Dr. G for the purposes of this book. Dr. G began to ask how I was feeling and introduced herself a little more thoroughly; this was the first time I had seen her, but later I would find out she was also one of the medical staff, a doctor just doing her rounds. Dr. G spoke very softly and quietly, very pleasant and soothing; she actually gave me comfort.

It was a different approach, not the normal doctor who walked in, asked a few questions, said good night, and left; it looked like she took an interest in exactly what was happening in my life, so I gave her the time. The relationship between Dr. G, myself, and my family has grown since then. My mother often referred to her as Dr. Barbie because she resembled the ever-so-popular doll on every shelf in a toy store. We became somewhat of a family, a bond stronger than just a medical marriage. Dr. G was so involved in doing her job. I remember her even showing up in my room dressed in workout gear, a sweatshirt, sweatpants, and sneakers. She had been on a run for the night because she lived nearby in Bronxville and would stop in to see some of her patients if there was enough comfort and/or trust in one of the many medical physicians. I had lost respect for them; she definitely gained it back.

"You know, I guess one person can make a difference."
Stan Lee

She seemed to be a little different than the other doctors I had seen; she had tried some new variations of medical--or should I say pharmaceutical--cocktails to see if she could remedy the solution on the medical side, meaning my bloodwork did improve. I seemed to get a little better, slowly but surely; however, I still faced that something mentally was not right in my mind. I was ready to give this new doctor a chance.

Would I still have the will to get up every morning and follow a regimen of testing my blood sugar, taking my insulin, and eventually (when I got out of the hospital) following this routine? Or was it time to throw in the towel? I only knew that I had entered the hospital in October. Other than being monitored throughout this period, most of my time was filled with around-the-clock feedings to match my insulin requirements and put some pounds back on. Most who have spent time in the hospital rarely would rave about the cuisine or go as far as have it rated by Zagat. Three months had passed, and I had recycled my menu options probably ten times over. Monday was lasagna, Tuesday some kind of chicken smothered in a gelatinous coating-- and were they really serious about serving spaghetti in Ragu sauce, where the meatballs were mostly breadcrumbs? Come on. I might have lost my mind, but I was still of Italian heritage. When Thanksgiving rolled around, I played it safe, dining on PB&J; I was still hospitalized, so I wasn't really thankful, but I should have been because I still had some life left in me. Everything served from October to December that crossed my palate tasted the same; much like my attitude, no additional flavor to the food or my personality, same perspective on life. I just wanted to attempt to go AWOL and rid myself of this ratchet place, where it still didn't register the amount of time and effort put in by doctors and family to bring life back to a lost soul.

It was already Christmas Eve; during this time, things had taken a turn for the worse. The numbers on the charts were abnormal for their desired ranges; blood sugars were unstable, the complications increased, and there were days when the neuropathy was so painful it hurt to walk or get out of bed, clenching my fists, which were much like my legs would cramp just to roll; just the everyday simple movements became a task. When the pain had passed my threshold, much like the master manipulator I was in college, I would coax the doctors to prescribe me pain medication. They often offered Tylenol (extra strength), codeine, and anything you could probably purchase over the counter, but that was not good enough for me. I wanted the hard stuff; I wanted to close my eyes, sleep, and forget about that pain, to the point that I didn't exist. Once the doctors were convinced, they began to give me oxycodone and other pain meds like morphine and Percocet; all said to be highly addictive, and how true that was. The demand was obsessive, causing me to sleep most of the day and eliminating me from having to remember the environment which I now call home. Once the doctors were onto this, they would sometimes still prescribe it--but only at night, in hopes that I could get a good night's sleep if that were still possible, seeing as my mind was in overdrive and the frequency of when a nurse would enter every hour on the hour, finger stick for blood sugar, and cuff for blood pressure and insulin if needed. Over those three months, things continued to get worse, and any attempt to bring my body back was feeble. I was malnourished, losing weight, dehydrated, and it seemed my body was giving in. At the request of my parents, they asked that one of the local priests or nuns come to say a prayer.

"Do not pray for an easy life; pray for the strength to endure a difficult one." -Bruce Lee.

Give me the hope, through the Lord Jesus, that I make it through the night, one more day of the month. I was being given my Last Rights at this hospital, and at this point, nothing was worth trying; at this point, I was no more than a medical zombie in a similar situation to hospice. I could hear people come and go, maybe relate to the voice, but not be sure who they were. I felt like I was in a dark room, blind. I could not see, just make out shapes with silhouettes of the bodies entering my room, but I knew they were there. I knew they were talking, but I wasn't sure who the person was. Sometimes I felt hands on my hand, holding them firmly, and lips against my forehead, kissing it gently. What was going on here? Was this it? Was I down and out for the count? During one of these occurrences, I remember a hand touching mine and someone saying something briefly something that sounded similar to a prayer; the words' Lord Jesus' were definitely used in one of the phrases, and out of nowhere, I felt a splash. It felt like a raindrop hitting me in the face. I had no idea what it might be, but I later discovered it was holy water; they gave me my last right to live in peace. Ironically, I did not die. I continued these days in the hospital, day after day, night after night, doctors in and out. This time, I was making a comeback... was it the holy water that gave me a spark of life? Was it a prayer? What was it?

"The power of prayer is still the greatest ever known in this endless universe." -Stan Lee.

My will might have been coming back; that fighter I used to know had no answers, but I was definitely aware I was feeling somewhat better, stronger; but still, I was confused... what was keeping me alive? Why was I still here? Who was still keeping me here? Was there a reason? I had so many questions, but nobody to answer them because nobody knew the answers:

"I have been up against tough competition all my life. I wouldn't know how to get along without it. " -Bruce Lee.

Christmas approached; a decision was made: my family was to bring me home in whatever state I was in. If I were going to die, I would die at home with my family in peace and on common grounds; miraculously, the recovery continued.

I think, for the most part, just getting out of the hospital was a plus: it gave me a little more sense of motivation to push forward and try to become myself again. I began to draw and write as therapy; they seemed to kill time during the day and allowed me to escape. I chose not to use the many vices of others, like drugs and alcohol. My way of venting was through a pad and a pen; just for those ten minutes or maybe even an hour I would write or draw, my mind would be in another world--a good world. I'd see the positive and be creative; that was who the real me was.

Now finding myself living back at home, under the care of Mom and Dad, I still felt controlled; I couldn't be my own person, so denial set in. I led myself to believe I had no such disease and no reason to attend to its needs. I needed some sense of my own stability, no caretaker, no doctors; I needed to be more responsible, an integral part of this healing process:

"It's a mistake not to give people a chance to learn to depend on themselves while young." -Walt Disney.

We continued my medical protocol with doctor's visits as an outpatient, constant med adjustments, and the addition of therapy; However, I was not healed, and far from being under control, I at least found myself being able to function in this world as a young adult who still had some dreams and promises. The question was if I would ever get there; when I met these goals, would I be strong enough? The doctors and my family were doing all they could to make me hit this point in life; it was up to me now to continue this search for sanity. If I were unwilling to endure the prescribed regimen by doctors and our medical team, the plan would fail. It was up to me to make up my mind. Do I want to live, or do I want to die? What's more important: who will I hurt or who will get hurt? I had to think about the others who had cared for me for so long: my mother, my father, my brother, and the doctors who put in their own blood, sweat, and tears.

CHAPTER 8: WRONG PLACE AT THE WRONG TIME

During one of the many staycations at Lawrence Hospital, the physicians concluded that after several losses in my weight, the practicality and need for treatment were all associated with the lack of eating or refusal. In layman's terms, I was being diagnosed as "bulimic" or "anorexic." Although my mind wasn't working at full capacity, and I can admit that I had used those chocolatey treats called Exlax a handful of times, I knew I was not one or the other regarding the doctor's diagnosis. As a result, I was taken by ambulance to Cornell Medical, which had an in-patient clinic that dealt strictly with eating disorders. Little did I know that I wasn't just being shipped over for some medical testing but would be a bit more than I expected.

My parents and I exited our vehicles and made our way through the entrance of Cornell, where we were met by one of the hospital administrators. Things seemed normal; we continued with a brief interview and physical exam; the rest was just the normal protocol, like patients' rights, insurance, etc...

The one major difference I did experience this time around was that when asked to remove my clothing for the physical exam, the assistant to the doctor proceeded to check my clothing pockets, and the exam was a bit more invasive. The only thing left out was being asked to bend over, cough, and assign my orange jumpsuit. At that time, I didn't think much of it; having been through this protocol numerous times before and not feeling in the best of shape physically or mentally, I was just going along with it accordingly.

When I was finished in the exam room, I was reunited with my parents, and we sat for a few minutes, just the normal jargon, and he entered. When I say 'him,' he looked somewhat distinguished, dressed in a suit and tie with a hospital badge hanging from his neck. We didn't have much conversation except for his introduction as an administrator of the program at Cornell and the exchange of names. That was when the shit hit the fan! Both my parents stood, so I thought, so should I; boy, was I mistaken. The dialogue from my mother still echoes: "It's time to say goodbye, for now, Chris." I thought, "I know; that's what I am doing." What was implied was my parents were leaving, but I was being checked in as a patient at the medical facility. I had a tough exterior and often could hide things, but like a reservoir, I felt tears descend down my cheeks and a rise in my temperature. My threshold had been met, and I became combative.

Once under control, my parents were escorted from the facility, and staff accompanied me to my room, or I should say 'holding cell.' It was a single room with minimal furnishings and baby-proofed; in other words, nothing was near with which I could possibly harm myself.

As time passed, nurses gradually made their way in and out of rooms; in other words, there was no privacy, but it was a little less frequent than at Lawrence. Food trays did make their way into the room at various times of the day, as well as some visitors I'd never met before.

Those visitors were other patients at the facility who respectfully knocked and introduced themselves. Despite the courtesy, the last thing I wanted to do was make friends; I just wanted to return to my safe place, alone, isolated, and not bothered. One of my favorite metal bands, Iron Maiden, summarizes just how I felt at that time within one verse and chorus of their many hits:

"Many years ago, I left home and came this way. I was a young man full of hopes and dreams. But now it seems to me that all is lost and nothing gained. Sometimes things aren't what they seem. No brave new world. What became of the man that started? All are gone, and their souls departed. Left me here in this place, so all alone. Stranger in a strange land. Land of ice and snow. Trapped inside this prison. Lost and far from home."

After I had gained perspective on the facility, my interpretation was that these kids--because that was all they were, had literally been checked in or left behind by their families and under the direction of the facility--were programmed to be robots. The kids woke, bathed, interacted, and even used the facilities (bathroom) simultaneously, as if big brother from the George Orwell novel *1984* were watching. One thing I knew for sure was that that would not be me, but how would I get out of this situation? The nurses were inattentively rude and often remarked that I refused to eat. Little did they know I wasn't eating due to not wanting to; rather, any time I did, I would feel nauseous, even at times get bad diarrhea and be unable to hold things down. Dieticians began to give me things like bananas and Susta-Cal (meal replacement; not being highly educated in endocrinology, little did they know my sugar was escalating higher and higher.

When I think back to it, I rarely remember finger sticks at any time of the day, yet they just kept trying to feed me. One of my immediate thoughts was to contact my brother, try and explain what was going on at Cornell, and explain that he needed to get me out of there. I even asked him to contact my cousin, our family attorney, to do whatever was needed to spring me from the chamber of horrors. Now looking back, I regret doing so; little did I know it was not their fault or responsibility. I was there, and my family was looking out for my best interests, but my mentality was not seeing it that way. My thought process was that I was being put here for a problem I created and was now paying the price.

"When you hear a recording of your own voice and begin questioning who you really are?" -Anonymous

Luckily something must have clicked with the physicians at Lawrence and my parents; I was released, knowing I was not in the right place, and we needed Dr. G back in the picture at Lawrence.

CHAPTER 9: SPLIT SHIFTS

After an almost instantaneous decision, mainly decided by my parents, it was confirmed by my appearance and state of mind that I would not be returning next semester to the college dormitory. The doors weren't closed on education, but any classes would be attended on a local campus where I would return home each day. At this point, my physical and mental state was worsening, and my attention span for just about anything was fading.

"This is your life, and it's ending one minute at a time." - The Narrator, Fight Club.

My parents were still supportive and explained they were there for me, whether it be school, work, or just taking a brief postponement. Honestly, my interest, or lack thereof, overshadowed everything that was going on in my own little world, including diabetes. Much like my life, time was rapidly passing by, and it was time to decide.

It took some time, but I got a clerical position with our local government system, which entailed working with the public, records management, and filing paperwork. By this point, my mind was not as sharp, and my temperament was changing; I often didn't have the patience to deal with the numerous questions from a customer on the phone or in person. This temperament also became apparent among my coworkers, who could tell I had a lot going on outside the office. Still, I was often given a pass due to my medical condition. It wasn't too long before the excuses I used to use at school started to spill over to work. I was sick and couldn't come in, running late, and sometimes I disappeared for periods so I could vomit, pee, and even find a quiet corner to nod off.

Miraculously, I managed to keep this job, mainly because I was a summer intern, and it was just temporary. The job wasn't much, just paying $5.85 an hour, but it was local, kept me busy, and was not very demanding, or so I thought. Most of my time in the office required being on my feet and dealing with the public, being able to answer relevant questions, and performing minor clerical duties. I played the role of a civil servant. I worked the summer hours from eight in the morning to four in the evening, then made my way to school. Class began around 5 p.m. I can remember trying to choke down a quick bite right before class or just binge on snacks from the vending machine on campus, which really aggravated the control of my blood sugars. Still, I chose to ignore it to get through my day on this rapid schedule, but it only lasted so long. I found myself severely fatigued, missing work the next day, and frequently napping in the middle of the day. Something else I began to notice was my extremities, like my ankles and feet. Binging on salty snacks, with blood sugars being out of control, allowed my body to swell in these areas; by the next day, the water retention would relieve itself when the water was back in balance with my body, all this due to the poor control of my diabetes. I could no longer continue at this rate, and my employer was gracious enough to grant me leave to address my medical condition. I later would learn a rumor had started in the office that the kid from filing may have gotten really sick and died well; they weren't totally wrong because, little by little, my body was shutting down, and most

47

of the water imbalance I experienced was due to the early signs of my kidneys shutting down.

On the other hand, the school could have been off to a better start; a summer graphic design course I was enrolled in became an off-and-on place to go, but if I completed my assignments, the professor was satisfied. The school was about twenty minutes away from home and took place in the middle of the summer when each day was over ninety degrees. One day I arrived early, feeling overheated, and wanted to find a comfortable spot to rest before the beginning of class. And there it was: located right inside the school, at the end of a desolate hallway, were stacked couches waiting to be removed from campus; perfect. Each Thursday, I would return to campus and find my spot, lie down for a while, and often doze off--thereby, you guessed it, missing class. Again, my mastery and manipulation would kick into gear, and I would manage to coax my professor into giving me a passing grade, primarily based again on my disease and the fact I happened to be extremely gifted in the arts and graphic design.

At the end of the semester, I found myself free from school and temporarily unemployed, still being supported financially and emotionally while under the roof of my parents. I found myself alone again, weak physically and weaker emotionally. Yet the way I was wired, I saw this as normal or temporary, something I would bounce back from. Failing to see the development of a vicious cycle, a victim to mind over matter. I failed to realize to make change a reality, I needed to be an active part of my conscious, pulling me in the opposite direction. Not by choice, it was time to invite an outside source into the picture. A professional with a non-biased opinion and skill set to deal with individuals in denial, depression, and confusion about surviving the demands of life.

CHAPTER 10: DOCTOR WILLIAM J

It was time to start therapy by addressing one part of the puzzle we had not explored yet, and that was my mind. What made the wheels in my mind turn? How was my brain working? Why did I do the things I did? Was I trying to harm myself or help myself? We needed to start somewhere.

Based on a referral from another doctor, we found someone in Manhattan; although the drive was not the closest, it was a start. I started fixing my brain, trying to figure out what needed to be changed, modified... anything to help me start thinking straight, thinking the right things, doing the right things, and just being myself again. For the purpose of this chapter, I will just refer to the doctor, or should I say psychiatrist, as Dr. William J or William. Initially, my mother would schedule my appointments, and we'd trek down to Manhattan together. I'd be dropped off at 10; after my appointment, I'd be picked up and returned home. At the time, this seemed very convenient, but still, I lacked that sense of independence. It was something I should have been doing on my own; my mother and father also needed pieces of their life back. After the first two appointments, I decided to make this travel independently, which became a challenge. You see, Williams' office down in Manhattan had very limited parking, and that was half the battle--finding a spot and making his appointment on time. The first few trips down, I thought I was the luckiest guy in the world. Never had a problem with parking. I'd leave, arrive on time, and wind up in Williams' office as he clicked the clock to start our session. Needless to say, I really wasn't so lucky. I was unfamiliar with the city and unfamiliar with a ruler called 'alternate side of the street' parking. I guess that was why each time I left Williams's office, a nice white rectangular piece of paper was sticking out on my windshield. I got a parking ticket. Even though I was unaware of this rule for Manhattan parking, my mind still told me, "I'm parking here; I'm not walking six blocks to get to this man's office. I'm tired, fatigued, and out of breath. I need water."

It sounded like I had not even begun the marathon, but I was preparing for it; if this wasn't enough, William's office was also located above a retail shop where his office was six flights up. Each time I entered his office, I would have to mentally prepare myself to make that journey up those stairs. Would I make it, did I have enough breath in my lungs? Did I want to attempt this, or did I have a choice? One step after the next, I made my way up, feeling exhausted, thirsty, sweating... you would think I just put in a 30-minute workout. I took my time, paused, regained myself, and continued. It wasn't that it took me that long to get up the stairs, but it was what it took out of me to do it.

Each time I knocked on Williams' door to enter his office, I looked flushed, winded, and basically out of sorts. Williams' office was typical: it had the brown leather couch; behind it sat his chair, and the office was decked out with other furniture and furnishings that looked like they were pulled out of a catalog from Raymour and Flanigan: very stiff, very professional--actually, very cold. I already got the impression this was not the place for me; our early sessions were really just trying to get to know who I was... things like occupation, things I liked/disliked, there were any hobbies. He covered the normal questions asked by a psychiatrist just so he could get into my brain and figure out a little bit more about me and how he could approach the situation. Once again, my creativity stepped in.

What I really wanted to say to this guy was summed up perfectly by a Rihanna and Eminem duet:

"I'm friends with the monster under my bed/Get along with the voices inside of my head/You're tryin' to save me, stop holdin' your breath/And you think I'm crazy, yeah, you think I'm crazy."

I know! Let's do the old routine, the college routine. I was actually very good at it by now; I could manipulate just about anybody, have them believe what I say and do, and have them fall right into my hands. So, ask away, William; I'm an open book.

As our conversation continued, it went very amicably. We traded some stories. I gave him some information, and I filled out our time slot. It was over. I made it through our first appointment and now let him do his homework. I don't want to address every session that William and I had, but things changed one particular day. William went from Dr. Jekyll to Mr. Hyde; the questions he was asking turned very negative and dark... he was trying to find out things that I had not exposed before. I didn't like his approach and became combative. At one point in the conversation, William saw that I was losing my patience.

I had met my threshold. He even asked, "I bet you want to call me a hook-nosed Jew?" H-hooknose Jew, what the hell is that? I knew William was Jewish but hooknose... I have never heard the expression. I let it go. I knew it was negative, but I just let it go. It wasn't worth it again; I could feel myself losing patience, just wanting to get myself off that couch and out of that office. After the hour, things had somewhat resided, became a little calmer, and we could depart from each other on a more positive note; however, I was not looking forward to our next interaction. William suggested I bring my glucometer to test my blood sugar together; strike one, I did not like testing my blood sugars or pricking my fingers at my own convenience or any others' request.

Strike two? He wanted to see the active log kept in the glucometer memory. Each week I would visit where he would review my numbers; he was a psychiatrist, not a medical doctor. He was not my endocrinologist; who the fuck was he? I'm not showing him these numbers. I know what these numbers are. I know what they mean: I'm out of control. My sugars are up and down like a rollercoaster; I'll tell him if he wants. He doesn't have to see an active log.

But again, I was in denial. I wanted to be like everybody else. I ignored these numbers, so finally, strike three: William was out. I would no longer see this man who called himself a psychiatrist. I felt like I was under the bright lights being interrogated. This would not happen again. Williams' last question on that particular day was: did I ever use chicken blood to test my blood sugar? I thought to myself, *Chicken blood? I know what he's talking about, but how does he know?* Were my parents aware of something they passed on to William, or did William ever have a patient that had done it before?

Feeling paranoid about the question, I started to think I was being put under constant observation in the hospitals and at home; I even contemplated if my parents had installed baby monitors at home to record my actions. As for the blood of a chicken... you see, my father was Italian and loved to cook, and one of his favorite things to do was make chicken cutlets once a week. At least. He would take out the chicken cutlets to thaw from the freezer; due to the time process, the chicken would leave blood behind. One day I became curious: does a chicken have the same blood as a human? It does look a little lighter. What does it have for sugar content? Does it have the salts that we contain? How would the blood sample register on my glucometer, and how would I get it onto the test strip? You see, the mind is a funny thing, and when you're in denial and out of control, you have a mental block, manipulation kicks in concerned with the outcome and not what it entails to get there.

My desired outcome was the only thing I was concerned with, i.e., showing good blood sugars, showing I was in control; if I could show I was in control, it would feel like I was being accepted or patted on the back for doing a good thing. Praise was what I craved; although I did not agree with William much, he was right this time. I was using chicken blood. I was drawing chicken blood from a package of chicken cutlets with an insulin syringe and placing it on a test strip. I found that chicken blood does register on a human's glucometer, leading to lower blood sugars at any time of the day. Not only was I getting good samples, but I was also creating a log for William to review. Little did I know at this time, being a bit uneducated on diabetes--or should I say, showing little interest in my health--that there is a certain test that is done to compile a three-month average of blood glucose levels; the hemoglobin A-1 C literally will average all the blood sugars taken over three months; it is then given an average, which is compared to values on a glucose chart, 7 or below being the norm for an insulin-dependent diabetic. I was averaging 13. Remember that these averages or values are unlike getting the high score in Mario Bros. The idea is to have the lowest averages or values; mine were quite the opposite; I was losing in this game. Long story short, I would not return to Williams's office at this point; our relationship had been broken. I did not appreciate how my situation was being handled. What made things worse now was that William-- and my parents, in my mind--were working in cahoots together to figure this thing out. What happened to my privacy? What was being leaked out? I thought things would only be disclosed regarding what was happening within his office. I began to lose trust in everybody again; feeling alienated, I'd have to do this my way

Walt Disney said it best when he made the statement:

"Togetherness, for me, means teamwork."

Sounds good, especially coming from Walt, one of my most respected entrepreneurs and humans on the planet, though my mind still could not understand this theory or thought; to me, it was me against the world. Nobody was willing to help me; in other words, I just wanted them to fix me. I didn't want to go through all the steps it took to complete this process. I just wanted to see the end product: fix and make me healthy. I want to fit in again and function in the real world without any hindrance. I don't want to look back on the past. I don't really want to worry about what will happen to me in the future, but I do want to live for right now... is that possible? The answer probably was that I could live for right now if I were more willing to make the changes that were being made by the physicians, or suggestions given by the dietitians, and basically taking the medications that were being prescribed. Do you see a lot was up against me at this time? I was still young at heart; I was in denial. I wanted my freedom from this disease; I didn't want to be told what to do and when to do it--not only that, but most people also don't realize when something is wrong with you physically, your mind paints a different picture. It allows you to think differently, see things differently and influence decision-making.

My perspectives at the time were all screwed up. I couldn't see what other people were saying. How would I fix this? Who could put my views and my perspectives back in the right focus? Where would I go next? Well, the obvious answer was that there was still the mental piece of the puzzle that needed to be addressed; it definitely was not going to be by William, so we needed to continue the search for somebody who fits my personality better, and we finally found one who did. I can't say that Dr. S cured me, but she made me feel a bit more relaxed, a little bit more like me, a little more comfortable in my skin, and she had a different approach: meditation.

CHAPTER 11: WHITE LIGHT

So, who was up next? Who was the next psychotherapist to try and pick my brain, or should I say fix my mental status? I say that jokingly but very lightly because I knew I had a problem that needed to be addressed. It was just that I wasn't in favor of psychotherapy; they say for psychotherapy to work, you have to be a believer, and at this point in time, I was far from it. I can at least say there was one benefit to this therapist, and that was that she was located locally, somewhere where I could just take a five-minute drive, park my car, and enter her office--with no steps, I might add--and see her for my appointment. This doctor I would see had a long name, hard to pronounce; I called her Doctor Dr. S.

I arrived quickly and on time for my appointment; when I entered her office, there was a strange smell... something I had smelled before reefer. Smoking pot? I needed to investigate.

As I sat in the waiting room, taking in the aroma of what I thought might be pot, I waited patiently; slowly, the door opened, and out came a tall, fairly husky-build woman with a very deep voice. "Hello Christopher, my name is Dr. S." Despite the appearance, her voice was subtle, actually soothing; she spoke pleasantly, and was very inviting, so here it was time to introduce myself to my new friend or, in this case, possible enemy.

Dr. S's office was dimly lit, and the smell that I thought was reefer was just incense burning in the background. It was very tranquil, and I preferred this atmosphere to William J's office. Dr. S did not ask me to lie on the couch. Rather, she asked that we just sit and chat for a while. She had the standard questions. What was my name, what did I do for a living, what type of things I like... this, like, you know... the whole battery of questions. I was happy to answer them. None of them were too investigative, just the norm. One of the most difficult questions she asked me was why I was there for the appointment. You see, I had no answer to this question because, at the time, I was in denial; I couldn't admit I needed help. I didn't know how to say, "Yes, I'm here, so you can help me fix my brain." I didn't know whether to say I was here because my parents sent me or a doctor did. I didn't have an honest answer.

Dr. S was very accommodating, noting I had no answer for her, so she continued to explain that although she was a psychotherapist, she used different modalities in terms of helping her clients. She wasn't the typical psychiatrist who made you lay on the couch and spill your beans as if I were at confession; she explained that our conversation would be loose and the topics would be about just anything. We were just here to talk and get things out in the open, seeing it was our first appointment. I still had not gained the trust of Dr. S and still felt her out as a doctor trying to pick my brain and get inside there, see what made my wheels turn, so I did have my guard up. She explained that she would like to try something with me today, something a bit different than the typical; she said it was called meditation. Dr. S used one of those clocks that portrayed soothing nature sounds, like rainfall or crashing ocean waves; it was relaxing and peaceful. Outside of that, I felt comfortable dealing with the doctor. I was trying to convince myself she showed interest and concern in improving me, mentally challenging me to compete in this cruel world again.

"Mediation is not spacing out or running away. In fact, it is being honest with ourselves." – Kathleen McDonald.

The first thing I thought of when she said meditation was a monk or a woman sitting on a yoga mat; I'd heard the word but never partook in it. This was something new to me. Open to her suggestion, I followed her instruction, and the session began. Dr. S explained: I would hear a series of bells. She asked me to focus on those bells, close my eyes, and just concentrate as if nothing else were around me... nothing coming in, nothing going out. I would be in my own little world. Wow, that's easy because I *am* in my own little world. I don't let anybody in. I don't tell much of anything to anybody. Perfect, let's do this.

As the bells began to cling and clang, I felt quite relaxed, almost falling into a trance. I was isolated, alone, in the fact nobody was there to help me but myself, and I was in a safe place. This was very comforting to me. Outside of being fatigued and tired from the diabetes being out of control and the out-of-control blood sugars, I slowly began to feel myself become sleepy as if I wanted to drift off, maybe take a nap, so I decided to go with it:

"Empty your mind, be formless. Shapeless, like water. If you put water into a cup, it becomes the cup. You put water into a bottle, and it becomes the bottle. You put it in a teapot, and it becomes the teapot. Now, water can flow, or it can crash. Be water, my friend."- Bruce Lee

I can't tell you if I did fall asleep, but I knew I was in a pleasant place. My thoughts were clear. My mind was empty; it was just a blank slate; that was when the inevitable happened, an experience I had never felt before. It was as if my body were displaced, hovering above the one on Dr. S's couch. I thought, "Did Dr. S possess the same magic as David Copperfield? I was now elevated above my own body. I could see down on myself. Why was I there? Why was I alone? Oh, wait a second, was I? I felt a presence, not one but two entities, one to the left and one to the right; I wasn't sure what this was, but as we continued the session, I felt and understood who and what this was: this presence was people of the past, people close to me, my great-grandmother, my uncle... there were no voices, no communication, just that feeling and then lighter feelings of peace, happiness, and reassurance.

You've heard the story about the white light; I'd come close to it before this was something very similar, yet surreal. Better depicted like white fog, a portal to another universe, I was consistently being pulled back from it as my body approached this portal. No fear entered my mind, and I was determined to cross into this space. Continually I was pulled from this portal as if to say I wasn't ready to enter it. It wasn't time to be introduced to the other side. My great-grandmother and uncle were letting me know that it was OK. They understood what I'd been going through.

It's hard... it's hard to get by each day, dealing with the problems I deal with and having no control over what my mind creates, but they also told me in their own way that it was not my time to pass through this portal. There was much more to give, much more to see, much more to learn, and much more to appreciate in this life. I felt like I was in this odd trance for hours, but when I came out, Dr. S assured me that it had only been five minutes, confirmed by the clock she kept alongside her. She asked how I was feeling. My reply was 'refreshed'; what I meant by refreshed was my mind had been cleared for that 5- to 10-minute, clear of any worries, any stress, or thinking about anything making me anxious; it was like five minutes of pleasure. I was in control.

I only had to worry about myself, and my thoughts were positive. I saw the world from a different perspective. I saw the good; I saw the opportunity. I saw what I could possibly be, to live a better life in these five minutes. I did not have diabetes. I did not have to prick my finger or give myself injections. I was just a normal being, functioning in the real world... no distractions, no medical issues, just a normal guy enjoying a normal day, not just surviving but living life.

Sessions with Dr. S did not last very long; after a few weeks, my time was over. I was not ready to go back, and once again, my mind began to take over; there was no need for therapy. I could handle this. I had got this under control. Again, for therapy to work, you need to believe in it; let's just say my brain was not convinced.

Before leaving the appointment that day, Dr. S would always make herself available. In due time, if I did return, she would teach me the techniques of meditation and be able to utilize them--not only within an appointment environment but on the outside as a method of release and escape.

CHAPTER 12: INTRO TO LOVE

With the frequent changes diabetes can have over you and its effects on anything from your health to your personality, I started to feel an urge in my testosterone and curiosity for the opposite sex. Until this point, the only woman figure in my life was my mom, who was basically my caretaker to this point. As I began to re-surface into the social world with work and school, I also developed a sense of need in other areas, like companionship, a possible confidant, and of course, at some point, intimacy. The scariest part was I didn't even know where to begin. For years, I had been the boy in a bubble, isolated from the world, a prisoner to my disease. It was time to break out of this shell, begin to experience the next stages in life as a young adult, and try and find the right one to spend this time with.

I was a shy guy, inexperienced, and I didn't have much social experience regarding the opposite sex; the only thing I did know was they did appeal to me. My hormones let me know, and I was ready to give this a chance. Much like everything else in life, opportunity doesn't always present itself; but you need to go after it when it does. On the other hand, some of us also believe in fate, and if something were meant to happen, it was; that was exactly what happened. Over the next couple of weeks, I ironically found myself constantly crossing paths with a co-worker; it was very innocent, but at the same time, I was very curious and interested. Again, I was shy, but what better way to create conversation than through work? Addressing a subject that dealt with our office, I was new and learning the ropes. We were briefly introduced, and I tried to creatively find out more along the way. I knew she was my senior by about five years, had been working at the office for about a year, and, oh, by the way, was married. Innocently we began to go on breaks together at work, talk briefly and then return to our desks, but it was obvious we both showed an interest in each other. It was also obvious through brief conversation we were both going through some personal issues. Before we knew it, we were sharing not only on breaks but lunchtime together, where I would always prepare something the night before for us to share the next day. One of these days, it finally came out: "I am having problems at home; things aren't working out." TJ's marriage was ending.

I hate to sound evil or facetious, but those words were welcomed by me, and I suddenly felt a purpose and hope for waking up each morning and showing up for work. One day I told her:

'I didn't come into your life to create added stress; I did to help you escape some of it. Yet at the same time, I am also here for you because I truly care and understand your reality. Let's face it: we live it, breathe it, and face it every day we wake. It's not about weekend rendezvous but about learning about each other. Again, baby steps. I will never be perfect, but I am learning as we go along. I am piecing together this puzzle each day we text, talk, or send pics. We are never completely prepared for what life brings, but we are stronger at approaching it, coping, and dealing. I am not going anywhere; you found a guy who may get disappointed but not angry, a bit naive, and sometimes looks at the glass as empty, not full. I've been to battle and back, and that's what I am here for: not only you but supporting everything you do.

Things moved fairly quickly, and people soon began to notice the attraction at work, so why not just go with it? Before I knew it, I was traveling thirty minutes after work to see TJ, much of which started innocently: movies, dinner, and conversation; we were grasping whatever detail we could in learning as much we could about each other. At this point, I had broken the ice with TJ and explained what medical issue I was dealing with and the complications it brought with it. Maybe I was too judgmental, but none mattered; she just saw Chris, the one she shared meals with and was co-workers with. Amazingly, I was finally fitting in! I felt a sense of normalcy, and more importantly, I began to replace some of the nurturing I always received from Mom with the nurturing style of this new bond I was forming with colleagues. I felt a bit of freedom and maturity and a little more self-confidence. But there was still something hovering over me like a black cloud with the complications and neuropathy I had. This was something I had issues dealing with. How would someone other than a family feel about being involved with someone who struggled physically and mentally with a disease? Would she understand and accept the added burden or end the newfound connection?

CHAPTER 13: DOCTOR W

How ironic is this: the time had come, literally. Things were going well between me and TJ; we continued to see each other every week at work and not only on weekends. We spent some time at a movie, at her apartment dinner, or any place, we could just share some quality time. Needless to say, we were both ready for the next step. You guessed it: intimacy.

Here I was, the 24-year-old virgin, not knowing what to do, how, or where to do it. Not only did these questions arise in my mind, a new one was standing in the way of the next step of our relationship. You see, at this time, I not only had questions about how this part of the relationship worked or transpired, but I also had questions about why my junk wasn't working. Yes, I said it: my junk due to diabetic neuropathy. Diabetes presented many other problems but neuropathy set in in areas I would have never expected. What do I do? How do I explain? Who do I turn to? I was so lost, embarrassed, and so insecure. I suddenly felt like that 15-year-old child again, fat and ugly, unwanted, and not feeling too good about my position. Another obstacle arose when I thought life was accepting me and everybody around me was accepting me. How would I handle this? Who would I turn to? I could think of only one person, someone honest, truthful, supportive, and who would definitely know what to do: Dad.

It is extremely hard to open up in such a situation. I felt embarrassed and insecure, but I needed to do it. I needed to address this topic if I wanted to proceed in a relationship and follow through on something I wanted so badly, not just the experience of lovemaking but continued success and continued progress in life with somebody who meant so much to me.

'The bugle has sounded; however, I am not at attention, my little soldier, pointing in quite the wrong direction. Am I awake, or am I asleep? My eyes are wide open, and I begin to weep. This has happened once before; usually too tired, I roll over and snore. This time I woke up; something was not right; my manhood was not ready to put up a fight. I even rub down below, give a small tug, my shoulders I shrug. Could this be the time? Am I the one who has lost the feeling, the warmth of the sun? Please, dear Lord, give me the will, don't make me turn to that magic blue pill.'

Moving quickly, Dad and I pursued someone who we heard positive views, somebody who had dealt with this, somebody who fixes things. The problem here was I was already at the point with TJ that we were ready to do this. We were ready to engage in this momentous occasion; yes, intercourse. Well, successful at this time; I managed to keep the sexual drive between us alive for some more time. I managed to put it off for a bit more. It was time to meet the specialist, Dr. W. You see, Dr. W was not only an infertility specialist but also a specialist in male performance.

The day I was introduced to Dr. W, I was met with questions, concerns, goals, and what I wanted to see, pursue, or transpire in my relationship. Basically, he had the normal questionnaire: diseases in your family, your age, your weight, etc. All familiar answers to questions I had been asked before. I'd provided this info so many times before that I probably needed to start carrying it in my wallet or bring my own personal file.

Now came the fun part, or lack thereof. Dr. W began to whip out all these different gadgets and throw all the different percentages at me. My thinking was a bit skeptical, but I tried to be optimistic. After discussing my options, Dr. W explained we needed to do some testing at home. I left the office with a black suitcase about the size of a large carry-on, walking out of the office that day. It was obvious not only to his female staff but to every other guy in that office that I was going home to test my little buddy.

Now while it looked bad and a bit embarrassing, I can't say that I wasn't glad I put myself through all these different exams. Procedures and questionnaires have allowed me to become more educated on myself and realize the condition was treatable and that the world has not ended. That night, I was a bit nervous, sitting on my bed with this black suitcase, a little uneasy, but I needed to put my mind at rest. I was told I needed to strap the side wrappers to my junk and let it do its thing as I slept through the night. It sounds scary, but what it really was doing was just testing to see if, during the middle of the night, my shit, basically, would come alive. All this would be detected by this medical apparatus.

The night was long; let's just say I was extremely uncomfortable. I know I didn't feel any movement through the night, but apparently, this device records every little motion made, and this was to be reported back to Dr. W the following week.

As a man, we know a woman's preferences (not to say all of them) and that size matters. At this point, that didn't even register in my mind, and I thought, who the fuck really cares? My concern was: would I be able to "rise" to the occasion if the opportunity should present itself? It was like a comparison between a broken finger where I could put a splint on, thus keeping it stiff and healing. Even if I were undoubtedly impressive in size in that area, what good was it if I could not perform with rigidity and to full capability?

Each night, that ritual continued: strap it on, pull it off, strap it on, and pull it off... did I know what was going on? No, not really, but I was just doing the stuff Dr. W. had asked. I needed answers. When the week ended, it was time to return to Dr. W with that all-inclusive black suitcase that apparently documented how my manhood behaved throughout the night and if it was possible to fix the problem I was experiencing. After Dr. W's staff had studied and reviewed my recordings taken from this black case, it was determined, no, I was not impotent, such a relief, but experiencing symptoms of low testosterone and ED. Yep, ED: erectile dysfunction; again, two words I've heard and two words I feared. The worst nightmare a man could ever hear about his privates and manhood is erectile dysfunction and impotence.

In a nutshell, no pun intended, Dr. W explained that many men experience this issue--not only me but many men, especially those aging and ones with medical conditions, which would be me. He explained that diabetes had created a lot of diabetic neuropathy or nerve damage; unfortunately, some of my nerve damage had gone to other extremities, other than the tingling in my hands and feet, and now my joystick. I remember hitting rock bottom; the bottom line: it doesn't work; how do we fix it, and how do we fix it now? Very calmly, Dr. W explained he'd been through this probably a dozen times; he further explained it to me. There were various medications for handling situations like these; it was just a matter of trial and error 'til we could perfect it. He tried to explain that if you were really in love, your partner would expect and accept these things. I'm 24 years old, and he told me that; my first time as a virgin was going to be under the influence of a drug--not natural, not beautiful, not spontaneous, a preplanned ordeal.

How do you react to someone telling you this at that age and that it was your first time being in love? The bottom line was if I needed to do this to do what I wanted, we would make it happen that day in the office. Dr. W introduced me to a drug called Edex. This sexual stimulant wasn't something you ingested or took through your mouth, swallowed down, and like magic, a boner; the supplement came in a vial, with which I would use a syringe. Yes, you heard it: a syringe.

This syringe, which I was accustomed to through using diabetic injections, was identical in size, shape, and the way you used it; no problem, I got this down. I know how to use this. What I didn't know was that to do this, the syringe, after being filled, would be directed directly into my shaft; yeah, directly into the weenie. Would I be able to do this? Not sure. As I contemplated, Dr. W told me he was ready to go. He returned to that room with a prefilled syringe and said there were some movies and reading material; I thought, great:

movies and reading material. Sure, that will excite me, but would it distract the fact that I was still sticking something directly in my shit?

Oh, what a relief when he told me that I wouldn't have to inject this miracle medication; that relief was temporary when he said, "I'll do it, much like Mark McGwire and Sammy Sosa competing for the home run record." The addition to EDEX could be comparable to using a corked bat to hit home runs, only with my apparatus. My Louisville Slugger became rock-hard, and I would last longer; and though unorthodox, I'd be more productive in the bedroom… maybe this wasn't so bad.

I closed my eyes, laid back, dropped my drawers, and felt a slight pinch. Nothing was happening. What was going on? He said to relax, it'll only be a moment, and before I knew it, I was left alone in this room where I suddenly felt this urgency in my pants. Some things were growing fast and hard, almost as if out of control. I hadn't experienced this feeling in a while; I became excited and fearful. I wasn't sure what to expect next?

Next: magazines and movies. Yeah, now I knew what they were for; here goes. So, after about 10 to 15 minutes, I did my thing. This was amazing. God, I don't think I'd ever been this hard. At this point, I felt like I could T off and make the ball hit the green in just one stroke; unfortunately, the stroke wasn't my problem. Something else was transpiring, and this really put a scare into me.

I sat there for 10 to 15 minutes before I realized things were working well, but I was ready. Yes, you guessed it, I was ready to explode, and the only problem being was nothing was happening. Where was it? Why wasn't that immense relief felt after emptying my ammo? Some time passed, and there was a quick knock at the door.

I covered myself quickly and said come in. It was Dr. W who quickly asked: how did it go? How do you feel? Was it what you expected? I replied, yes, it was what I expected and a bit more? However, the outcome was unexpected, and I needed some answers again. Dr. W was loaded with information and seemed to have answers for everything: percentages, situations, remedies, etc. I started to explain, and before I could even finish, he gave me an answer: retro-grade ejaculation. What the fuck was retro-grade ejaculation? I knew what the word 'ejaculation' meant, but I only knew it didn't happen this time. He took the time to explain that in diabetics, or anybody experiencing nerve damage, the nerves have a tendency to shut down; so rather than holding things tightly or being able to push things forward, my nerves were weak and damaged and acting in reverse. Yep, the reverse; so, whatever I expected to come forward was going backward, being brought right back to where it came from. In this case, my bladder.

The doctor explained it was just that it wouldn't leave my body; wow, now this opened up another can of worms. I guess I could look at it as built-in birth control, seeing as my fish couldn't swim upstream, but I also felt an immense need to unleash the forces that built up inside my body. Truly, at this point, the only thing I was interested in was performance, making my partner happy, and feeling good about it--not only for her but for me, sharing in the intimacy, feeling relief, excitement, all the good things that came along with being with your partner. On the other hand, pregnancy was not an issue at this time, but later on, it would present itself in a life-altering matter. So, as I was still frustrated and my little friend still standing at attention, I continued with some questions, most of them answered, some of them not again. I'd have to go through some trial and error and experiment with this new solution to my problem-- most of all, how would I introduce this into a relationship with my partner? Will she accept it? Will she turn me away,

Once I was ready, things had deflated, meaning I was no longer aroused; I left the office with a handful of prescriptions. Some questions were answered, and I was somewhat ready to move on, at least with myself and the experimentation of this wonder drug. Time passed, and I continued utilizing my newly found drug addiction. It did give me the ability to get an erection. However, these erections lasted for three to four hours. What, three or four hours? I was just looking to have sex, a good time, and a little enjoyment with my partner. Now what do I do? How do we resolve this issue?

I quickly dialed the phone and asked to speak with Dr. W; again, he was calm. Sudafed, he said. Sudafed? I don't have a cold? My nose is not stuffed up. What did he mean? Dr. W briefly explained that Sudafed would constrict blood vessels in my penis. Meaning it would stop the blood flow, bringing down that erection and bringing me back to my normal size. I can't lie, although it sounded like this would be the greatest thing in the world, be aroused, be up for hours, and please your woman, but when the pain was throbbing after being erect for so long presented itself? It was definitely not a feeling of pleasure but more suffering.

It finally became time to not only introduce this new process into my life; I also tried to introduce it to my partner; just how would I do this? Would I be able to sneak it in? Do I tell her? What would be the easiest way to go about doing this?

I wouldn't know until I tried; this was the night, and it was time for me to unveil the new me, the one who was able to perform, the one who was able to hopefully satisfy their partner, the one who would hopefully finally experience what he had waited for 24 years. That evening, TJ and I got together for a nice dinner and movie, and after that, yes, this might be the first time... the first time I had to unleash this new weapon. Would it work? Do I have the confidence to try this, or do I just avoid it?

The evening was moving smoothly; dinner was good. The movie was funny. The conversation was great, but I felt the mood swings were moving toward that area of intimacy. Should I get myself ready to do this? Should I take the time to step away and inject that miracle drug? I was nervous, very nervous, but I needed to try. I'd been embarrassed before; nothing was different... so what if it didn't work? Would I walk away with my head between my legs, defeated again? As I had said earlier, TJ was a bit more experienced, not only in years, but I'm sure, in terms of intercourse and sexual engagement. She had been married for a bit and, I'm sure, had been through this situation before; I guess what I was really saying was, "Let's just kick back, try and enjoy, and let her hold the cards," and that was just what I did. Things advanced quickly, and the next thing I knew, I found us together on the couch, kissing, hugging, and all the good stuff it came down to.

Would this work? At this point, I was excited, and I felt somewhat of a sensation down below, but not the necessary amount for me to make any kind of contact or penetration. I did start to feel a little embarrassed. What do I do to avoid this? How do I get up? How do I run away? I don't know what to do. TJ handled this like a champ; almost as if to ignore it, we found other ways to amuse each other. Keep ourselves pleased and entertained, and enjoy the rest of the evening.

After this brief session, TJ put some light music on. We shared some wine, and she asked if I wanted to explain or discuss it. It was probably the last thing I wanted to hear at that point, and I really wanted to explode or blow up. Still, she was giving me the open mic, the stage, my chance to explain what was happening, why it was happening, and how I could fix it, so I took the opportunity.

I took some time to explain not only diabetes but what comes along with it-- mainly neuropathy, in this case. I dug deeper and tried to explain what I experienced when involved in a situation like the one we were just involved in. She seemed to get it; she seemed to want to know more. It was as if it really didn't matter what we did. It was more important that we spent time together, enjoyed ourselves, and appreciated each other's company for now. I was good with that.

I felt a bit relieved, but it was still there in the back of my mind. I was broken; I didn't work properly. I couldn't fix it. I had some workarounds, but I didn't have any answers. Would

I want to try this again? Would I want to put myself through this? I wasn't sure, but she seemed to be the one who was there, willing to take on whatever challenges I brought and willing to bring her in and take on whatever challenges she brought. The support for each other was developing, and we pursued that.

As our relationship progressed, TJ and I found other alternatives and how to pleasure each other, which was fine and definitely enjoyable; but I still had a built-up frustration, anxiety, and insecurities; I had inherited diabetes; much like anything else, it was something you had to attack head-on, not put aside, and continue to try to fight it. Like I said earlier, trial and error, so that was what we did. Little by little, each time we met, we might introduce this magical wonder drug and see if it worked, see how far we got, just taking it one step at a time.

Eventually, it did work. It seemed like it was all part of the process; however, we still lacked a lot of spontaneity, and a lot of times, this area of intimacy had to be preplanned--not my first choice, and I'm sure not hers. What was once new now became old. It was as if it had always been part of this relationship. We were both getting used to it. We worked with it and got through it at this time. Nothing really stood in the way; my feelings were still mixed daily. Was she still wanting to be with me?

Ultimately, I realized there was much more than just sex; there was also experiencing life together.

Something we found in common came in the form of a mouse. Yes, I said a mouse: we were both huge Disney fans and couldn't be more excited about it. We brought up times when we went on trips with our parents and friends, but there was never anything quite like Disney. You could be a kid again, but nothing else mattered to you in the land of make-believe; in this land, you would be young again, disappear into all the innocent things in life. We appreciated being out there and looked forward to going back to that park each and every day. I had never experienced that in my life. Health-wise, diabetes was there each and every day.

I couldn't escape it, no matter how hard I tried. And when my eyes weren't opened? It was there with my eyes closed. It was in my dreams; I just wanted to free myself of this burden, and this time around, I had support from someone other than a family member, and it felt so natural and nurturing.

TJ soon learned traveling with diabetes wasn't the easiest thing to do, but she was a planner. She planned all this. Making sure we had an answer for just about everything or at least a Plan B. Nothing, not a thing, was missed when TJ planned a trip, which made me feel comfortable. I was ready to rock, roll and go on these trips and experience life thinking like free of diabetes, free of stress, and most of all, sharing it with someone I loved. I could probably go into about 5 to 10 chapters in this book, writing about our days at Disney because that was about how many times, we returned... some good, some bad. We did run into some problems, but we worked them out. Overall, Disney was a safe haven, just us and a mouse, kids again, living life as it was meant to be: no stress, no worries, just a day in the park.

That being said, along with these good times, TJ and I were getting even closer; when I say closer, I mean wanting to be together, work together, or "let's get together tonight or on the weekend," more so like "let's get together and live together," eat together, sleep together... basically let's get married. Questions arose; again, I was a little bit younger. She had been married once before, and was I ready for this? Was I ready to introduce a new person into my life? Would she be able to handle her hardships? I brought the diabetes, the good days, the bad days, the doctors, etc. I was still mentally functioning like a kid because I had lived under my parent's roof for 24 years. I had everything done for me, and again remember I was that boy in a bubble. I had to come up with a solution, a decision. I wasn't being forced, but I was ready to move forward. I was going to do it. The question was: how do I do this? Where do I even begin? Do I just ask her? Do I prepare for this? Do I have enough money to get married? Am I socially ready? Mentally ready? Physically ready? There were so many questions, but I was in love. I think that overcame everything. Now that I had taken my mind off diabetes, it made me look forward to what was possible and inevitable, like more complications with the control of my disease.

CHAPTER 14: BONDING

TJ and I wanted to be closer on the map, so what would be our next step? She lived way up the line, and I was down here at the other end of the county, and one thing we did share was a standard workplace, not a place to return home after a long day's work. After serious consideration, she moved from her neck of the woods down to mine and rented a small apartment in the same town. Right then, times were rough: she had just gotten divorced, money was tight, and she was leaving her circle of friends, support, and people she had grown up with for years. How would I make this move on her easier? What steps would I need to take at that point? I really was unsure. Could I juggle this task and be on top of Diabetes and its control?

This was my first real relationship. I had never been put in this situation, but I would do my best to listen and learn. The day came, and it was time. TJ made a move, and she was settled closer to me, closer to work; we were happy because we had more time together and easier access to see each other; stress was evident and getting bigger, but despite the stress, we became stronger. Our relationship was still a struggle at times; as a result, something had to be done; moves needed to be made. Again, the question was on my mind: would I be ready to let somebody into my life who never experienced living with someone dealing with Diabetes or a disease? Was I ready to share all I came along with, or would she be second-guessing?

There were just so many questions... Decisions had to be made for the battle, and understandably the types of topics that would lead to a life together, like planning a future.

Money was tight on both ends. I was still a summer employee where we both worked, and TJ, newly divorced, was on one paycheck; we needed to come together as a whole, more than just friends, more than just partners, more than just boyfriend and girlfriend, but possibly husband and wife. Where do we start? We didn't live together; we were both struggling to make payments. What would be the next step? Marriage?

I was nervous, extremely nervous. I had never been alone; I was isolated for most of my childhood, as compared to John Travolta in the 1973 classic "The Boy in the Bubble." I had loved my family and friends, but not much more than that, and now I was ready to let somebody into my life. Somebody to make a future with, and memories and plans. I decided to be put in a course of action; after I popped the question, where would we get married? Who would come to the wedding? Just how would we do this? When I finally got a set of balls to do it, pop the question. I couldn't think of a more perfect way: why not have a mouse marry us? No, I don't mean to have him actually marry us; but why not do it in the environment of the mouse? Disney. Even better yet, let's do it on the open seas.

That year we planned a trip. I had never been on a cruise and was ready for the experience—we would board that ship as partners but depart engaged.

CHAPTER 15: THE WEDDING

Despite the stress, we seemed to have things figured out, had everything down on paper, and were ready to let the world know what we were ready to do. It seemed like every time, we needed to make a decision, we were always under a time crunch. We needed to get this done and get it done soon. At this point, it would've been where and when we wanted to move in together. Would we stay local? Would we move somewhere else? Just where would we wind up? We wound up staying in my hometown; we found a place after looking around. It just felt right after viewing so many different apartments.

This was the one. It was a little out of our income, but it felt right, so we said let's do this. Let's bite the bullet and make this purchase weeks before marrying and tying the knot. We still were not physically in this apartment. No couch, no rugs or appliances. Basically, the bare minimum. I had not officially entered a so-called "living in sin" phenomenon. So now that we said let's do this thing, let's get married, we focused on where? Should we have a big wedding? A small wedding? Should we then get married in a church? Where would we do this?

Plenty of discussions went into this, and eventually, we decided we wanted a wedding--something small, quaint, and family-oriented, but something to be remembered. Something we could share with our loved ones and share together; we were lucky enough that I finally made somewhat of a decent salary, as was TJ. We now had a dual income to save some money, and we were even lucky enough to get the ability to work overtime; our goal was to pay for this wedding and do it our own way, anywhere, from the photographer to the cake, to the music that was playing the day we got on that dance floor. It was our day, and we were going to do it all.

When the summer rolled around, all 98° of it. The day moved fast. We spoke with many friends; it was a blur, but I think we did well. I knew everyone had a good time, and they let us know it; however, the world is somewhat ironic in the sense that we put out a lot of money into making this wedding happen and, in the end, ultimately came out with no more money than what we put in. But you know what? Everybody had a good time. We were happy and ready to begin that new life together. Just one last thing before the night ended: acknowledge Mom and her love and dedication to getting her son through the many medical mishaps; I grabbed the mic and took the floor:

'Some time ago, I, as well as my family, began to deal with the many issues dealing with my diabetes where ambulance rides to the hospital became so well known, a second home. I saw the white light, this light, a place I would confront my fear. At this time, I could not understand and often felt guilt for the situation I had created for my family. Today I stand here before all of you present a mature man and say I understand the reason for that white light. The light is for those who have passed and those of the present; it symbolizes the strength they gave me, the ability to stand before you today. So, Mom, take my hand, hold it tight. I thank you for adding more strength to that white light. Tradition says for the mother to dance with her son exploring the relationship between her and her young. I have chosen a song representing our relationship and the support and love I received from you. So, listen to the song; the words will describe the woman there to help me survive. Despite so many songs, only one will be chosen with the words I have been unable to say; however, it will be heard in the song soon to play. I never really understood the meaning of a song, but there is one that has gotten through. If I were to use her words, these would be the ones I choose. Though this song is only meant for two, I still can't forget Dad, Michael TJ, and my immense love for you. Tell me, Mom, what you see; yes, it's the same little boy you taught to read. I can now only share with just one on this special day, so please take my hand, and listen closely to the song to be sung because these are the many reasons for who I have become. Mom, you will always be my strength, my inspiration.'.

In the back, the guests start to sniffle, tissues drawn, and the lyrics of Celine Dion start playing, "You are the Wind Beneath My Wings."

Now with a sense of freedom from everything except employment, we decided to go on a honeymoon. Our choice? Why, of course, Hawaii. It was probably one of the most educational and enjoyable vacations I had been on; the flight was long but well worth it, and the return home was much needed. I felt homesick and displaced, but I was ready to pick up where we left off now as Mr. and Mrs. Romano. Things, in the beginning, weren't much different. We still worked together; we came home, shared a meal, went to bed, and started all over. It was like Groundhog Day, but we had each other. What would be next in our game plan, and what would we do? What were the plans? I was not sure, but I didn't know. We still had to get up each morning and go to work, much the same as we had done for the past two years; it seemed like the honeymoon had happened so long ago... did it really happen? Was it a dream?

Yes, we were living now in reality, not separately but together. We needed to get through this thing called life together. What was the next step in life? What was always perceived of the normal relationship? What was the norm when you got married? Yep, have kids. I mentioned earlier that TJ was a bit ahead in age and probably itching a little more than myself to bring some little ones into our lives; I, on the other hand, wouldn't say I was against it... but much like a marriage, I wasn't sure if I was quite ready. I still felt like a child; my "bubble" only popped briefly ago. I never really thought about it at the time, but that black cloud was still out there: how could I have children if I couldn't function correctly--especially in the bedroom. How would I allow myself to have the ability to give my new wife the opportunity to become a mother? We both knew I had difficulties, all complications due to diabetes. Who would return to help us with this? Dr. W?

During this time, TJ had a niece. We spent much time with this niece, cared for her occasionally, and helped raise her in some sense. We enjoyed doing it; she was our own, and we treated her like our own. Were we ready for our own? Not sure, but I did enjoy having the ability to spend time with this little person. Love her, feed her clothes, bathe her... did I want this for us? I think I did, but I remembered we gave this little tiny miracle back to her mother at the end of the day. There were days when I loved being a couple like her parents, but I was just concerned about TJ and having another mouth to feed, another body to come home to and pay attention to, other than ourselves. My freedom as an individual was short; my freedom and exposure to a new life with a new wife was short; would I want to jump right in to bring a new life and new responsibility? Someone who depended on me because they were too little to understand or function in this world? I had many questions at that point in our life, but we did this together. TJ explored all our options, and we were going to make this happen.

CHAPTER 16: ONE SHOT DEAL

Well, you guessed it. How does the saying go: first comes love, then comes marriage, and next comes baby in the baby carriage? This was definitely known not only to me but TJ as well. We had a lot to consider when making this decision; let's face it, the cards were basically stacked against us. I had my issues with diabetes and getting my fish to swim, and TJ was a bit older, presenting a smaller window of opportunity with added risk. Seeing she was a little bit more advanced in age, we again sought help from the professionals. The guys who knew all the answers or the woman who understood all the sensitivities; actually, we needed both. Where the hell would we begin? Do we know anybody who may be going through this? Was there actually a doctor who specialized in this? It wasn't just my problem or TJs problem; we both had a problem. We needed to start to investigate and investigate soon.

As far as we knew, TJ was functioning properly, so most of the time, the focus was on me, where I stood. Would I be able to comply with supply & demand? Would I be able to take this opportunity and make the best of it? We had approached many doctors searching for help conceiving a child, even the best on Park Avenue in Manhattan. All with the same response: "The odds are not in your favor, and it's quite expensive." We did have insurance, but it was impractical for any of these top doctors to accept it. We spent a lot of time outside the offices in the city, crying over the information we received, thinking that we probably just needed to take the extra steps in the process. However, having a baby was probably not in our future. We were given options of adoptions and even sperm donors, but we both wanted to raise a little creature of our own, made from our genetic pool and not some stranger we knew no more than the cabbie who drove us to the office for the appointment.

'Now, an embryo may seem like some scientific laboratory term, but the embryo consists of unique information that defines a person. All you add is food and climate control, and sometimes the embryo becomes you or me." - Todd Akin (Author)

After processing what we had learned that day, whatever soul and hope were left wanted to escape my body. I wondered if TJ had felt the same. I had made many promises when becoming her husband, including "In sickness and health." If I were in her position, would "in Sickness" become our worst enemy in this marriage? Was I preventing her from meeting one of the most desired milestones in a woman's life, becoming a mother? How do I react to knowing I may have stripped the women I love the opportunity to create a new life and live through their child's eyes? I knew I was looking far ahead, but I was becoming extremely insecure and vulnerable, considering the situation I felt I was placing us in.

I began to feel guilty; this was all due to my issues, not TJ's. I could feel her emptiness and wanted to isolate or run from the situation, much like I did as a kid with diabetes. I knew I needed to be strong for both of us, utilize the education we received today, and take it elsewhere. We were in this together, and we needed to continue the persistence of bringing happiness into this world and our hearts as expecting parents. Who else out there could I ask? Why not Dr. W?

Not only was Dr. W an expert with male hormones, but he was also a fertility expert, especially when dealing with the male side of the problem. It was a little different this time, as I approached Dr. W not alone but with my partner, my wife. Why not? This was something that definitely involved both of us, something we looked forward to doing but just didn't know how to do. Bringing a new life into this world... where do we start?

Upon first arrival at Dr. W's office, he explained he had been through this before, a much-expected answer, which meant I felt a little more comfortable that day. We mainly addressed my issues, diabetes, and retrograde ejaculation.

Dr. W basically spelled it out: your little swimmers are getting held up behind the dam, and it's due to your neuropathy. This damn doesn't open, allowing the release of these little swimmers into the ocean; basically, he was telling me my sperm was being ejaculated but backward, actually into my bladder. No harm to me but more complicated to conceiving, or should I say doing my part naturally in fertilizing my wife's egg. How would I get my sperm to her egg? How would we make this thing hatch? Dr. W explained one way or the other, we would manage to get what they needed from me, whether through extraction, medication, or other means; we just needed some brief testing and trial and error. I'd been down this road before to solve a problem. But I was s still nervous.

We began the process. I knew I had several options I could try, so we needed to begin several attempts at what would be the most successful or give us the highest percentage rate. We discovered the easiest but most invasive would be to actually go in, and when I say "go in," I mean to go in surgically; they would make a small perforation within my testes, sac, junk, call it what you want. First, it was needles; now, it's incisions. I guess I got to do what I got to do to get what we wanted, and I was more than willing. Now that we had somewhat accomplished a game plan in terms of how my body would work, how my body might respond, and what I needed, let's make sure that TJ was OK as well.

Her appointments began with fertility drugs, doctors, Q&As, and all the above, much like I was accustomed to. The issue of age came to the top. TJ was getting a little bit older, and the window was getting smaller, so we needed to move. She also began to see a specialist then; her name was Doctor K. Dr. K was a good doctor, actually TJ's OBGYN. She'd seen Dr. K for quite some time, but she wasn't the right person to handle the situation. Upon suggestion, we were given a particular doctor's name in this specialty, so our next step was to set up the appointment and see what we were working with. I remember going back and forth with the different doctors, even down in Manhattan, to the best on Park Avenue again. Occupying stairwells outside doctors' offices as we cried together, not knowing whether this would work or if we could have children. Topics like adoption or male surrogate choices would re-surfaced again. I wasn't the biggest on a male surrogate because I wanted to be as much a part of this as she did. Adoption… yes, always an option if the bottom line.

We agreed on an approach. We decided to start the process: a day existed of daily appointments. TJ had blood drawn to see what her levels were at for fertility. It was a constant back-and-forth for her from work to the doctor to the doctor to work. It was a lot on her. It was a lot on us, but we were dedicated and determined to bring a little baby into this world together; we had met our goals in determining where we stood through the blood work established.

We would have to introduce some medications. Yes, I was quite familiar with this area. Shortly after, TJ was prescribed a cocktail of meds to play around with her hormones, which meant yes, you got it: mood swings, sensitivity, being emotional, all of the above, but we were both ready for this. And did we have a choice? Not really, so we dug down deep and went with it. Medication classes had started, and we were both very well much involved. You could say it was an area where I felt very comfortable.

This was an area where I was well-understood, well-educated, and pretty good at doing it. I almost felt like I could administer the class we attended based on my own experience, which was great; now, we were a little bit ahead of the game instead of always being behind. Time was moving and moving quickly.

We continued our dosing schedule, changing dosages, upping, and continually modifying her hormone levels… at what point would we finally be where we needed to be? We were instructed to just sit back, and when those levels were hit, the next steps would be explained. The next steps were finally introduced; the object was to extract sperm from my body and remove eggs from TJ's body. At that point, one is introduced to the other and see if they would coexist. The process was called in vitro fertilization, or IVF. It was a waiting game again;

we were against the odds; we had a minimal amount of specimen as opposed to the norm they wanted, and the sperm still had to be extracted from my body. The rest was left to science.

I didn't even know how many fish I had swimming in my pool, but we were going through all the motions and doing what we needed to do to make this possible. Considering I was a good athlete, it was far from a game; we had one chance to make this work. It wasn't like throwing a dart into a bullseye or driving a puck past a goalie; this was the creation of life; it had to be spot on, with no fuckups or inconsistency. It was not like the trophies I had received earlier in life; this was humanity, the true calling admired and cherished by most married couples trying to conceive. Although my diabetes played a major role and presented some setbacks, I refused to let it influence my thought process. I wanted this new entity in the form of a child to have an opportunity to grow and experience failure, but at the same time utilize it as a mentor to others and make a difference in this world, which I had failed at.

It was sometime later that we received a call at work. It was the fertility doctor. To my surprise, TJ refused to take the call and handed me the phone. It was a female nurse, one I was not familiar with, and said, "Hello, Mr. Romano. I'd like to let you know where TJ's levels are." I can't even tell you what the number was or remember the number, but it was large. I didn't even bother to ask, but she continued: "Seeing as your numbers are this high, congratulation, you're pregnant."

CHAPTER 17: IT'S TIME!!

Now that the news was out and that we would be expecting parents. TJ and I couldn't have been more excited; tears filled our eyes. It took a lot of work and effort on both our parts to conceive this child; however, we were not done. Now we had to follow through with the most important part of the birthing process and protect this child in the room, ensuring it was nourished and protected and given the best opportunity in life. TJ and I were very determined, made every doctor's appointment, kept up with her medications, and documented everything we were learning about. Our excitement about being parents was growing, and so was TJ. She began to pack on the pounds quickly; all up front, people began speculating based on the shape and size of her midsection now blossomed. This meant wondering if it was going to be a boy or it was going to be a girl; we just knew that we were pregnant, and I had to continue to do what we were doing?

We were still working long hours at work? Trying to save some more money, seeing as a new baby is coming. We did start to look at things like cribs, carriages, bassinets, clothing, etc. I have to admit, it was a lot of fun. Both TJ and I were in agreement: we did not want to know what the sex of the child would be.

Here was the twist: we had been looking forward to introducing one child. But it was quickly detected there were two heartbeats. Yup, two heartbeats going on inside TJ's stomach; we were expecting twins. Yes, we would be dealing with double trouble; moving forward, everything was thought two times over, from cribs to the bassinet, extra clothing, and extra diapers... it was a bit overwhelming at the time, but also exciting. TJ and I never knew we would have twins in the early goings; we both strongly felt we would be blessed by such. I remember at some point in the process that these babies were growing inside, we had been informed of some bad news. TJ reached out to me at work, explaining that one of the heartbeats was fading almost undetected. They weren't sure if we could hang onto one of them; that got even rougher on TJ, physically and mentally.

I think the mental was the biggest part. How do you go about your everyday life, wondering if one of your babies will survive? What kind of thoughts go through your head? I can only wonder what she was going through, so I was there for support as we continued to monitor the growth and well-being of these two little guppies at this time.

The heartbeat was still detected and growing strong; time was moving fast, and we needed to prepare ourselves. Prepare ourselves to care for two lives we had never before prepared for; prepare for becoming a family. Doctors began giving us new numbers, such as early birth weight, premature babies, the date, etc. Fascinatingly, the new date we were given was February 14, Valentine's Day. Little did we know, TJ would go much sooner.

It was late in the day, and TJ and I were at work when one of my coworkers alerted me that TJ was not feeling so well; she was having labor pains quickly. I got to TJ. I managed to get her into the car. We drove carefully but aggressively towards the Westchester Medical Center, knowing we were carrying precious cargo.

The Westchester Medical Center was overwhelmingly large compared to the local hospitals where I stayed. TJ's OB/GYN had already been enroute to meet us there. Feeling anxious and nervous behind the wheel, I tried to calm myself as I pressed my foot down on the car's pedal, and it accelerated like a missile. I felt like we were breaking the sound barrier, only doing 55 in a 45, but we were on that mission to Mars--in this case, Westchester Medical Center. The only focus was getting to that hospital on time and safely; the radar of any cop behind a bush waiting was non-existent in my train of thought. Needless to say, not only were stop signs and traffic lights not in my thoughts, but neither was the Nissan Maxima stopped in front of us.

I quickly got out of the car and ensured the other person was OK. I apologized to him. We checked any damages; fortunate enough, none were present when he spotted TJ and saw her condition, meaning being pregnant. He said God bless you, and I wish you the best.

Once we arrived at the hospital, the staff started to prepare TJ and accommodate her labor pains. The pains went on for quite some time. Unfortunately, TJ was not dilating rapidly. We sat for hours, waiting and waiting to see if this would move on more quickly. The doctors even gave TJ Pitocin to help stimulate these contractions, yet nothing was happening; at this point, there was really no caution or need to panic. At this point, the doctor told me that it would probably be safe to go home, and there'd be no further stimulation or induction to move these babies along.

Considering the circumstances, it was extremely hard for me to leave. I gave TJ a quick kiss on the forehead and told her I'd be back tomorrow with a bag for her and anything else she needed; little did I know the doctor also told me to be prepared because 8 a.m. tomorrow morning we were going full throttle C-section. I didn't know at this point what was going through TJ's mind when she heard the word "C-section" but I knew she was excited to be a mother, and all that mattered was her babies being delivered safely.

Until now, we still did not know the sexes, nor did it matter. Surprisingly enough, I found enough to keep me busy that evening: washing dishes, packing TJ's bag, watching some TV... and surprisingly enough, before I knew it, I was back at the hospital, putting a gown on, scrubbing up and entering the room where my wife TJ lay, being prepared to welcome two lives into this world.

We were soon underway, and before you knew it, I was in an operating room filled with at least ten people. All surgical staff, five per baby at this point. Everything was pretty much out of our hands, with the doctors doing what they needed to do. I gripped TJ's hand firmly, leaned in towards her, spoke softly, and there it was: a cry.

We heard the first cry "You have a son." I heard another cry right behind, "It's a girl; you have a daughter." As quickly as they had the newborns out, they began to clean them up.'

'Here they are, each a tiny child; it's paid off. It's been all worthwhile. Two little bundles rolled up in their bed, little curls atop a tiny head. No longer dream or doubt; these two babies are finally out. One a girl, the other a boy, a little nervous, not a toy. We will love, feed, and protect you with care, although twins never compare. You will each be unique in your own special way; Mommy and I will never forget this day. For now, neither bears a name, but I will love you both the same. Today begins something new; Mommy and I are nervous about what to do. Mommy and I will pull it together; thankful for being blessed by two angels bearing 'the feather.'

The babies were in good hands now, each a little over five pounds preemies; it was time to make sure TJ was OK and get her fixed up. Before I knew it, one baby was going to the NICU, and the other needed to be fed.

I was a little bewildered as I fed my daughter. I wondered what was happening with my son and what they were doing to keep him in a different area. Apparently, our son was experiencing a bit of jaundice, and his lungs still needed to be cleared more thoroughly. I finished feeding my newborn, gave TJ the update, and was off to the next, where I found my son in the NICU; they were still cleaning him up. He was sunbathing under the lights, getting a tan to redden his yellowish skin but doing quite well.

Over the next few days, TJ and I had the babies in our room in their little bassinets, where we learned to feed, dress, and be with each child. I have to admit, I was a bit nervous; like any other new parent, I wasn't sure if I would break this baby, hurt this baby, or do something wrong, even with the simplest things like putting a little shirt over their heads being ever so gentle with their little chicken necks. But that was why we were there, preparing to take these two little angels home. Somewhat educated about their care.

Another thing we needed to put on paper, literally, were our babies' names and what we would refer to as they grew into these little animated people. We had a few ideas but nothing concrete. We decided to tear up pieces of paper with all the considerations scratched out on them and literally pick from a hat. In seconds, we had it: welcome to the world, Jordan Alexander and Julianna Alexis. We're your Mommy and Daddy!

The day we left the hospital, it was extremely cold, and snow was on the ground. I remember taking out the stroller for the first time, attendance front and back. The attention we gained at the hospital from ongoing patients or people just visiting with us was quite a good feeling, although nervous and engaging. From that point forward, it's safe to say you can only imagine the sleepless nights, the feedings, the crying, the laundry, the doctors' appointments, trading off one baby for the next... all part of being a parent. Although I would love to reminisce and revisit the many milestones made by my children and could probably write a book about it on its own, I will leave that up to them. Maybe someday they'll get the inspiration to write a book about their milestones, the goals they set out to achieve, how they got to where they are now, and how they survived what experiences they had at home. I would much more appreciate reliving their lives through their own eyes, how they thought, how they perceived that feeling... just what they felt as they grew, matured, and became the adults I am so proud of today. For that reason, I've reserved that choice for them. Now twenty and having lives of their own, they remain huge parts of my life. Out of respect for that and the probability of being able to write just a book on itself about the many milestones we have experienced together, I will leave you with two poems (one for each) that can be seen in each of their high school yearbooks:

'There will be days ahead where all has not gone to plan, regardless of the effort, too much on hand. To give up would be an option, or just walk away, but we know, son, that's not how you play. At this point, you must decide: should I fight or should I hide? Take a step back like you have done before, accept the challenge, and open that door. Take that chance to see what you can be, one step closer to earning that degree. Regardless of your decision, we watch with pride, for you are ready for what's outside. Jordan, we love you more with each day and have plenty more to say; but let's make it brief, the time has come to turn over a new leaf. It's time to let go for just a while, keep in touch, and continue to make us smile.'

'Where is that little girl we once knew? The one we dressed in pink and blue? Years passed very fast as we watched you grow. Could this be the little one we put in the ballet show? Of course, it's you, all mature, with all the confidence to endure. Your personality is so inviting, turning dull to exciting. We can only hope for all the best; focus on the school; we got the rest. You will hear many voices; we are confident that you will make the right choices. Julianna, your initiative will take you to many places and, along the way, many new faces. Now it's time to explore; don't be afraid to go through that door. We're still here, not too far; you're prepared to raise the bar. You are such a dreamer and quite artistic. Your view is so optimistic. We love you so much, couldn't be prouder, blossoming like a beautiful flower.'

CHAPTER 18: VOICES FROM BEYOND

It had been an extremely long afternoon. TJ and I were at it again, arguing over the simplest things, but just enough to create some kind of turmoil--unfortunately, in the middle of all this were our two innocent spectators, you guessed it, seven-year-old twins. Snow lay on the ground, and the temperature was unbearably cold, and all I wanted to do was get those kids home. One more stop and that might become a possibility.

On this particular day, we needed to make one more stop before returning to the apartment. TJ's car needed to be dropped off at the mechanic, located down US 1 in Mamaroneck. This ride always seemed like a journey, but TJ insisted on bringing her car there for service. At this point, I began to feel myself in a fog, somewhat incoherent, but it would come and go. I really paid no mind, feeling the way I did. The only smart suggestion I made on the day was for TJ to ride ahead with the kids in her car, and I would take mine. We would meet up at the mechanic. I let TJ drive ahead and made my way to the other vehicle. The first thing I could think of was I needed to eat; something I did not think of was that I had not done so all day, and my sugar was low.

I was usually pretty good at holding out on a meal; after all, it didn't require me to take any additional insulin or stick myself with any insulin syringe. Anytime I could escape the injection or finger stick was a pleasure, mainly because it made me feel like everyone else.

I put the car in gear and headed out, heat finally kicking in, music on the radio, and I was alone, at peace, for just enough time to breathe from that combative afternoon. As the heat got warmer, I began to feel a bit drained--fatigued; at some point, I even closed my eyes, thinking this would pass. The lids of my eyes continued to find a happy home being closed. It couldn't have been more than ten minutes into my ride before I saw a bright flash and heard a loud crack. The collision was hard and loud enough to startle me from my spell. The car was rolling over and over until it finally stopped. I sat upside-down, still strapped in, and all my car windows blown, outside to back. Ironically, I felt extremely calm, on top of it; I didn't feel anything like being injured. The cold air was blowing through the windows; as I said, I was trapped and couldn't get out.

Suddenly I heard someone approaching quickly: "I am a doctor. Are you OK?" I explain calmly, yes, I just want to get out. The doctor replied, "I don't want to move you until help arrives." While hanging upside-down, it was hard to comprehend, but ultimately, the doctor was right. Paramedics finally arrived on the site. And quite quickly at that. I began to hear them chatter back and forth: "Do you smell alcohol? Is there a cell phone on the floor?" After that, all I remembered was the sound of metal-to-metal, steel on steel: I was being cut out from the car, held back by a seat belt that crossed over my chest and heart. And we were on the way to the closest hospital.

I did not tell anybody for some time that a soothing voice kept calling me while strapped in that life-threatening situation: "You're going to be OK. You'll be OK." It turns out that, on the day, nobody reported any witness, no woman nearby... just the doctor, the paramedics, and later TJ and the mechanic. So, who or where was this woman? Where did the voice come from? When I finally arrived at the hospital, I was told I had snapped a utility telephone pole in half and rolled my car three times until it landed on its roof.

I can often look back and ask myself: Did I know getting into the car that day, something terrible would happen? Did I purposely crash that car in planning this? Did I intentionally send the kids with TJ, knowing there would be a fatal end to this ride?

I found myself in a very dark place at this time. I cannot dwell on the past. I can only ask questions about that cold winter day. I should have checked my sugar before getting into the car, but I did not. I was selfish and wanted to be like everybody else without eating or taking any insulin. It felt like the norm. Or could I question an attempt to end all the drama called life?

The takeaway was that day was my breaking point. I sometimes think partly I wanted to be like everybody else, but on the other end, was I planning something more drastic, like crashing my car and ending the pain I carried inside me? As you can see, many questions and dilemmas arose from this situation. The question still went unanswered. It was on a cold winter night. Who was this woman? Where was the voice coming from? Do we really have a guardian angel or angels?

'Have you ever felt like you were being watched? A presence so near, yet comforting, no fear, suddenly an emotion, maybe a tear, perhaps one we lost, one so dear. Your body remains still, but now comes the brisk chill. Like ice in your veins, the comfort remains; some might wonder, why not scream? Others are left with the question: is this a dream? We all have angels, believe it or not, clouds of emotion; they find your spot. If this phenomenon should present itself, take the opportunity, take the chance, it's only your angel in advance. This angel will visit day or night, bringing you strength to continue the fight. If you find yourself strong and ready to go on, take this opportunity and pass it along. We may not be ready, so ignore the greed and pass on this gift to those in need. The person may not be within reach, but with one quick prayer, we can preach and share the gift of love, for this is a blessing sent from above.'

CHAPTER 19: DISNEY DRAMA

Now, with kids in the picture, jump forward seven years. What's the most highly anticipated trip for most families with children? And where is the presence of a life-size rodent welcome in your home? You guessed it, Mickey! This would actually not be the first time for TJ and me. We had frequented the park numerous times and, at this point, could have been inducted alumni to the Mouseketeer's Club alongside Frankie Avalon & Annette Funicello. It also wasn't the kid's first time. We had visited when they were a bit younger, but this time we would take full advantage of their growth spurt, allowing them more opportunities to climb aboard the big girl and boy rides. The lines were long, and the sun was scorching. Both did wonders for my Diabetes. Between the hours logged waiting in lines, the profuse sweat that soaked our clothing, and the miles calculated walking to and from the parks, my blood sugar went up and down more than Mickey's runaway train. But it was tolerable, and I wasn't willing to have any setback due to my expense. Although TJ and I were just as excited (maybe more), this was all about the kids, providing a great experience and memories. Again, Diabetes got the backseat, and mind over matter would kick in. We were in Walt's land of make-believe, and Diabetes didn't exist.

"I don't wanna grow up" -Peter Pan.

On the other hand, Diabetes would play an integral part in this trip. Our fast pass to the rides and attractions multiple times. The theme park would accommodate its patrons with reasonable arguments or a handicap, and we would utilize this exemption like Willie Wonka's golden ticket. We gained access, moving to the head of the class in a line and out from the sun, ready to board a ride housed in an air-conditioned environment. Both kids, one more daring than the other, now had their eyes set on the most popular and thrill-seeking rides. You know, the ones where you get excited but exit white as a ghost. And that's just what happened. As we trek across the park, I found myself before one of the more historic rides, Space Mountain. I was excited, thinking, we get to board this makeshift rocket ship even quicker, no wait, no second guessing. Only fair there were 2 kids, so TJ and I would accompany them (I say excited very lightly). The 4 of us sat tandemly, one in front of the other, strapped in, waiting for blast off? I was familiar with the ride but still felt a little uneasy. I could see the excitement on the kids' faces, motionless and quiet, as they gripped the lap bar before them. A siren sounded to break the silence, and the ship we now occupy took off, reaching 0-60 in seconds. Our children, once dormant, now came alive screaming, waving their arms in the air, and laughing. I thought my kids were insane. Lights began to flicker, noises coming at us in different directions. The vehicle zig zagged to the left and right, everything but upside down. Upside down? Suddenly I felt like I was in a time warp. I was behind the wheel of my 2001 Toyota Highlander again, rolling repeatedly, no stopping this time. This was Disney. Where was my "Angel in the Outfield"? I was having a flashback. As much as my children screamed with excitement, I screamed in fear. I could feel the sweat drip down my back and my blood pressure rise, gripping tight to whatever I could. When would this nightmare end? After a 3rd lap, we finally came to an abrupt stop if that was not enough. I now felt like I had whiplash. We exited our vehicles, kids jumping up and down, and they ran ahead of TJ and me. I slowly dropped back, dazed and confused; TJ could see something was off and asked, "What's wrong?" I would explain later, but at that moment, I would've crawled up into a fetal position with nobody around. I regained my composure and joined my crew again, masking my vulnerability to the children like I did the lack of control of my Diabetes.

Science says roller coasters are examples of "physics in motion." On that day, the only thing physical was me breaking down.

"Whatever triggers you also reveals what you need to heal" - Anonymous

Day 3

With that episode behind us and avoiding the children bearing witness to a grown man (their father) losing his shit on an amusement ride, we stuck to our game plan. We had the magical pass, so let's hit as many rides as possible. Most of these rides were spread out, and of course, only right each child took a turn choosing what came next rather than what rides were within the vicinity (not my choice, but I went along with them to keep the peace). The time going from one side of the park to the other felt like Deja-Vu. "Didn't we just pass that? I know I've been here before?" Good thing we all had our new sneakers on because it was all about comfort, or so I thought? Throughout much of the day, my feet did feel a bit sore, yet tolerable. But that particular day, something was different.

Sure, both feet were hot and sweaty (attractive), but the left was burning. Again, letting the rest of my group walk ahead, I decided to stop and look. To my surprise, the sock, which once was white now a scarlet red. A blister not only formed but burst. Knowing the importance of foot care for Diabetics, I knew I needed damage control. But that would be another setback and something I didn't want my children to see. I put my sneaker back on, again catching up to TJ and the kids. We spent several hours more in the park before the return to our room at the Polynesian. By that time, it was too late. My ankle had swelled, bearing a resemblance to Fred Flintstone. Thinking ice would bring the affected area back to the norm, I settled in for the night in preparation for another long day. Morning came, and I woke to a 12-inch white line. No, not a line you waited on or drew with chalk but a vertical line going from ankle to knee cap. My luck (which I hadn't had much), the resort had a resident doctor available to assess this situation. After the doctor cleaned up the wound and made his assessment, he determined the line was an infection. An X-ray would be needed to eliminate any danger of invasion of my bloodstream or bone. The doctor suggested going to the nearby clinic. Not only did I hate being in hospitals, but my impression of a clinic was a place you check in but not out. And the staff was there to learn while treating the next victim. Sorry Patient. I wasn't going. "Please do what you can do here, and if it gets worse, I will go." What the fuck was I crazy? I was playing my Jedi mind tricks like I did in college now with the doctor. Not considering I could lose my leg from the knee down. A half hour had passed, and there was a knock at the door, "X-ray." Magically a radiology technician from the clinic appeared with a portable X-ray machine. We had to wait on the results, but in the meantime, I was prescribed heavy doses of antibiotics. Now exposed to my injury, the kids were scared, "Dad's hurt" I had to play the role of Superman (in reality Stupid-Man) and assure them I was OK rather than just accept the concern for my well-being. Again, with eyes on the prize and not considering the consequences, I had goals left on this trip. Aside from returning home with my leg intact to see my daughter dance with Belle and my son duel with Darth Vader. With four days left in the trip, it was a struggle, but the meds kicked in, worked their wonders, and fairytales did come true for the kids. I can say that I often wonder if I were under better control of the disease, would this have been so traumatic. But already know the answer...

"Be in control of the disease. Don't let the disease control you" - Anonymous.

CHAPTER 20: LIGHTS GO OUT ON BROADWAY

"I can see the light in the darkness, but only feel the dark in the light." - Elusive.

It was early on a weekday, and I was running a little behind schedule. As a matter of fact, I hadn't even crept from my bed yet. I looked over at the clock, the time a blur. By now, my bedroom should have been well-lit by the sun, and I could tell it was raining. I scrambled and finally pulled myself from the bed, tripping over a pair of sneakers I had tossed aside the night before. Much to my surprise, when I raised the shades, I still found myself in a fog, not the type after a hangover but a blur like a deer in headlights. Oddly enough, it was only on the left, and I figured it would clear.

I jumped in the shower quickly, where I lathered up and tried continually to clear this blur in my vision. Much to no avail, I was unsuccessful but needed to get to work. Driving the familiar road to work was a challenge that morning, as I used only one eye; I made it late, but I made it. The day progressed, and I tried to ignore the distortion in vision, but seeing as I work on a computer and read through legal documents, it was probably a good idea to put this aside and get my eye checked out. All I could think of was my boss saying, "He just got here, and now he's leaving," but after working in that office for 25-plus years and having personal time at my disposal, I couldn't care less.

I was already being treated by an ophthalmologist, so now it was just a matter of getting to her office and hoping she would see me. Dr. Sherry was always good about making time in her schedule, so I wasn't too concerned. After many scans, bright lights shined in my face, and after a couple more invasive tests, I was told that the lights went down on Broadway... well, figuratively. I would learn I had a TIA in my left eye and would need to address it with another specialist more familiar with it. "TIA" in laymen's terms: I had a stroke in my left eye.

It really registers quickly with your body when suddenly you lose one of the five senses, in this case, my sight. Much like Al Pacino in "Scent of a Woman," I started to rely on other senses to function somewhat efficiently each day; there were times I relied upon friends and family to lock arms and be escorted around, and other times I was left alone, a bit bewildered. During this brief loss of perception, I also developed a cataract in my good eye, so I was temporarily visually impaired. I couldn't tell the difference if I were in the company of a tall Victoria's Secret model who smelt so delicious, I wanted to take a bite or if it were a child chewing on a piece of Juicy Fruit. But I kept my thoughts and hands to myself, hoping the figure beside me would just say hi or "Can I give you a hand?"

Thankfully I knew that the vision loss in one eye was temporary and would return, but I found myself really appreciating the five senses functioning properly; by now, I had been examined for just about any complication associated with the complications of Diabetes. I am using the word respect because, due to the lack thereof on my part, Diabetes was not giving me respect back. Instead, I chose to ignore the valuable lessons I was taught through trial and error, and the disease was unwilling to forgive and forget.

Over time, the vision in my right eye was regained but still compensated for the left. Another trophy was awarded for my ignorance and mismanagement of my Diabetes. Another question would you have? Could have? But didn't take control of this disease.

CHAPTER 21: DILEMMA

"Should I stay, or should I go now?

Should I stay or should I go now?

If I go, there will be trouble.

And if I stay, it will be double

So come on and let me know." - The Clash

I can sympathize with the lyrics from The Clash, and that if I go, there will be trouble, and following, leaving once-familiar grounds in my apartment in the town I grew up in.

It was only the beginning; now, things had to be divvied up evenly: our first priorities were our children, their schedules, and how we would continue to support them as mom and dad, co-parenting. At this time, I felt it was the right time to leave. Seeing the children utilizing the apartment as a pit stop, their circle of friends, sports, and schoolwork constantly occupied their time. Now 17 years of age, the children were no longer looking to Mom and Dad for everything; they were more independent and had a better mindset of functioning in this cruel world.

The tension in the apartment only grew thicker. The children were growing, yet so were the pressures of living together. At this point, TJ and I had become glamorized roommates. The apartment became a place to wake up and return to sleep; outside that, it was just a roof. We were both providing over our children's heads. I can obviously not back the lyrics of The Clash, where it says, "If I stay, it be double," because I had already made plans to vacate the premises.

I remember approaching my mother and explaining to her briefly what was going on, what I needed, and what was a roof over my head. Most around us, like friends and coworkers, had no idea what went on behind closed doors. They saw TJ and me as this happy-go-lucky couple who went on vacations to Disney and had two beautiful children, raising them into two productive adults. On the other end, family and people close to us knew there was tension, and something had to give. The effects were taking their toll on both of us, physically and mentally; worst of all, we had two children stuck in the middle. It may come off as humorous, but I was starting to hear the voices again, this time not the demons I once knew. A little voice told me, "Get your ass out from under that roof. Staying there will only get worse for you and your mental welfare." I knew I had to remove myself from this toxic environment, but I still had to remember the two young adults who needed their father. How would this affect them and how they think of me when disappearing and dropping out of the picture? I sat down with both of them; at the time, they were already aware of the situation, and with their blessing, they assured me they would be fine; they realized I was not happy, and I no longer smiled. I assured them I would still be there for them 100 percent, but from a distance. Their reply was they would much rather still have a happy and functional dad as their mentor and voice of reason than some incoherent man who, although their father, was so dysfunctional he was unable to even take care of himself.

That was the blessing I needed from my kids--no one else, not a doctor, nor a friend or a parent, them. My two greatest creations. When I approached my mother and asked about moving back, the answer was not even a question and came without hesitation: "Christopher. This will always be your home."

We continued to raise the kids as if we were still living together... sporting events, school events, groceries, whatever was needed for the children were there. We were co-parenting, doing it successfully, but still at each other all the time. With the kids growing mentally and physically, the apartment was only shrinking. We were running out of room, time, and, most of all, patience and love. Money had been a major factor in the stress levels at home. TJ and I had never had joint accounts, only way back when for the funding of a wedding, and if you remember right, we never saw any reimbursement, just smiles and happy patrons at a party we provided back in June, summer of 2001.

One night it finally came out argumentative and loud, but that was how I felt my threshold had been met, and I was ready. I wanted a divorce. At one point, TJ even tried to salvage this from happening when we learned her parents had just become Mega-Millions winners and would be awaiting a large sum of money. TJ confided in me that her parents would be helping with the kid's college dues and that it should help alleviate some of the stress and issues we were dealing with; this did not register with me. As I said, this had just gone on for so long that I had met the boiling point and was ready. Remember, I was stubborn; I did it when I wanted something done. So, when I asked for a divorce, I would follow through.

We both needed to approach experts, the attorneys, who are basically out there to make a buck. I don't think they care how the decision favors their client or defendant, but it's their job, and they do it well. They play the role of a friend, employee, voice of reason, and advocate; however, their best role is that of a two-faced, money-hungry individual out for themselves. It was only getting worse if we thought we had bills before the divorce. These attorneys were expensive; they charged by the hour and minute. They didn't miss one talk that happened via phone call or email and were sure to bill it, accepting basically any form of payment with a credit card, debit card, cash, check, or money order... as long as they were being paid, they were going to invite your gratitude.

TJ had suggested seeing a mediator, which I did not favor. In addition to that, the attorney she chose happened to be somebody I had known for quite a few years. This disgusted me: I didn't want to be in the same room with this man, let alone hear his name; I was not going through it with a mediator. I was getting somebody to represent myself as an individual, solely for my benefit and the best for the children. Once we established who would, hopefully respectfully, represent each of us, we got the ball rolling and started the case. The first priorities, of course, were the children. Where would they live? What type of schedules do they have with their parents? Holidays, how their finances would be paid, and more. This went on, back-and-forth, back-and-forth between the attorneys. It got harder and harder to get a hold of these individuals. It became as if they were avoiding us, which led to more time, money, and no definitive plans for anyone's future.

I was doing my best, this time living under my parent's roof again. I was back under big brother's watch; my health was not improving. It was actually getting worse. The continued weight loss and kidney function was dropping steadily, the nights became longer, and my mind constantly questioned where I was headed, whether medically, physically, mentally, or financially. The divorce proceedings started out uncontested, meaning we would agree upon everything; nothing would be challenged or fought over... if only life were that easy. Continuous paperwork was produced by the attorney's emails and texts, things filed with the local county clerk's office, papers to be signed, things to read through, things to agree or disagree on, and it was so much. My mind was just in a whirlwind. Seeing there were still some questionable areas, some gray areas. We now needed to go before a referee, somebody supplied by the courts, to make judgmental decisions on what he or she thought was fair to both parties.

She was an advocate and supposedly mutual participant in the decisions or suggestions made for the plaintiff and the defendant. A response from this referee to a question posed by my attorney: it addressed my health and asked how his client was supposed to be able to, respectively, pay that amount of child support, considering the number of medical bills he not only had but would probably have in care-- if and when a successful place was found for him. True, he was playing sympathetic and trying to hit a sensitive nerve of the referee, but she wasn't going for it. She was well aware of both as a county employee such as herself.

TJ and I had very good insurance packages through our employer. She explained that most, if not all, of the needed care and attention for myself would be covered by the county benefits plan, and the standard formula for child support would be applied.

All this was pretty new to me at the time. I knew what child support was. I know why she ordered it, but I didn't know how they calculated it. Quickly I was schooled on that area: I would be responsible for 13% of my paycheck to go towards each child; now, if you do the math, that's 26%. To break it down even more, the county pays their employee's bi-monthly, meaning we get two monthly checks. After the support went into effect, I would receive one monthly check and be expected to live on it. If it weren't for being supported by my parents at this time and being provided shelter and food, I probably wouldn't be able to get by, nor would I have survived.

Much like I had done before, I started to forget that I was still diabetic and needed to control my blood sugar. This time would be rougher if I thought it was hard before. I focused on finalizing this divorce, and diabetes took a backseat to this priority. Ironically, we would eventually come to some form of agreement. I'm sure both of us would say not completely amicable, but doable. It is only fair to say that there are always two sides to a story, so to go any further or deeper into what transpired throughout this discovery phase of divorce would be unfair in making one-sided impressions or perspectives of what transpired to reach a matrimonial judgment. Ultimately, I feel it was the right decision, but at times I had second thoughts, especially when looking back on birthdays and holidays.

'It takes something special, something close to me yet so distant. A void in my life, my heart, and the air I breathe. I sit here alone every night; I cry out your name; you're not in sight. What happened to us? Where did it go? Our lives together were supposed to grow. I've made my mistakes and left them behind, hard to forget; they clutter my mind. Please continue to absorb what I voice, a true meaning, not just one night but whenever needed. Feel the words I now write, read them with an open mind; read them carefully, not blind. Been too many nights since we have spoken, shared a meal, or told a joke. It took a lot for me to call, reach out, and bear it all. To you and my family, I must admit, there were days I felt worthless, a piece of shit. I lived with demons for so long, monsters dancing and so strong. Those demons are gone; I do not regret ridding myself of the opposing threat. My eyes still weigh heavy, filled with emotion and salty tears like the ocean. You see, my love for you was never lost, paying the price at a high cost. I speak of love and sharing, just two souls always caring. We started strong, in it together; day after day, we battled the weather. We chose to add to our tree, creating life, a family we will be. Off we went to start our dream, not as one but as a team. One big question we would ask: were we ready for this task? The days were long, forever cold. Would we receive that call and be told? The news would soon leak; we both could hardly speak. Now we were blessed with more than one, now a family, daughter, and son. On that day we had shared, there I sat, no longer scared. Time would pass; it was only so; optimistic about how they grow. Over this time, I would slip, gradually losing my firm grip. The hand I once held, the moments we shared, lost for now, and I'm scared. They say time will heal. Put away the past. Life is short, just too fast. Again, it's just me here to show the man I can be. It's been hard and quite the task, but it's time to remove the ugly mask. Twenty years later, some time has passed, and a birthday wish to last. It's not too hard to guess my needs, a birthday gift; my heart still bleeds.'

Throughout this time, I still needed a transplant, and the numbers were dwindling, and my kidney function had dropped to 17%. The standard was 20 to be accepted into the donor program. Throughout this matrimonial process, I began to receive calls from donors. The calls were actually fairly educational, where you were given a profile of the individual who had voluntarily signed up as a donor and now became an actual candidate to give life to another, unfortunately, as a result of death. You see, this was my only choice at the time. Hope, I should say.

I had thirteen relatives and friends come forward, each tested and profiled, but no exact matches. Some were close but not close enough; some were too old, and some might've had a condition; it just wasn't the right mix for a successful transplant. At one point, calls came left and right explaining how the person died, similar to a brief profile, and if I would accept that organ. At one point, I actually felt as if I were back on a dating site, viewing profiles to see if I was interested in dating the woman in the picture; but in this case, it was no question. If an organ is available, you take it, say yes, and wait. What I mean by wait is when you receive these phone calls, it is just an initial alert to the fact that there was a donor; you were in the top three candidates or the top three matches being informed. You had to relax, sit back, and go about your normal day. If indeed you were the chosen, the one blessed to be given life from these deceased parties, you would receive a second call; if not, it would be no call.

This happened repeatedly, at least four times... but how could I relax? How could I just sit back? Each time they called, I got excited and nervous, yet not very optimistic. If my mind wasn't playing games as it was already, it was creating what I would call a "cluster-fuck" of emotions. The calls were promising at times, but at the same moment also provided false hope, but I had to see if I could maintain the positivity and optimism that my call would come. But distress was immense between the divorce, the children and their well-being, and waiting for transplantation.

CHAPTER 22: REALITY CHECK

This weekend would be a quiet one. My parents were traveling to Florida, and I would find myself a king of the castle, seeing I still lived in my parent's home. Obviously, not being mentally sound (and let's just say not comfortable in my own shoes), I often found myself depressed, alone, and again, isolated, all too familiar in my everyday life... although I needed a break from being under my parent's roof and, again I felt somewhat uncomfortable being alone. The house was quiet. You could hear a creek, you could listen to the birds outside, you could hear raindrops, anything that made a motion, you could sense. The crazy thing about this is, as quiet as it was, I found myself just fine, doing nothing... watching TV, lying in bed, sleeping on and off. My normal day. Sometimes peace like this can be a good thing. Your mind does need rest, especially my mind; it was always working overtime.

But looking at it differently, I had lost my protective barrier. My parents were gone. No one was around, and I found myself in a dark place. This was a place I had been before the common ground. Wheels turning, evil thoughts brewing. I started to think about the good times, bad times, things I'd been through, something I'd gotten through, and things that I had still been living with. I also felt myself go in and out of different spells, nodding off, waking up, tossing and turning, and being vulnerable. I remember even bursting into tears; these could start for a minute, stop for a minute, or continue for an hour. I really couldn't put my finger on what I was crying about, but I knew I was not happy with my situation. I had finally reached my boiling point, my threshold, where all that seemed useless like there was no return to normalcy. Like something had to be done to prevent this continued life of pressures. But were they really pressures? Were they really things that were so bad? Was it my mind that was making them be perceived that way?

I wasn't seeking help. I was in denial. I wanted out. I didn't think about the people around me. At this point, it was all about me; I just wanted to put an end to it all. The inconsistencies, the insecurities, the stress factors... would this be it? Would this be the night when I took that chance? How would I do it? What did I have access to do? I wanted to go easy, not painfully.

This time around would be different. This wouldn't be a futile attempt. This would be when I would close my eyes, never to be opened again, when I had finally convinced myself, we needed to move on and get this done. It came to fruition via insulin.

I have access to insulin. I had read about and even seen the famous movie about the doctor killing his wife by overdosing on insulin; that's how I'd do it.

I made my way down to the refrigerator, where I stored my stash of insulin. I usually kept two to three bottles on hand, just how many would be needed to do the deed. After I retrieved the bottles, or vials, of insulin from the refrigerator, I grabbed the bag of syringes and some nighttime sleep medicine. I had my arsenal and was ready to proceed. Before moving any further, I remember picking up my cell phone and recording a message five times over, each time with the same message. This would be the last time anybody would hear from me. It was something I needed to do. I could no longer deal with the pain and the pressure; ultimately, I would delete these videos.

Most people knew what I was going through. They didn't know the pressures and the demons I was surrounded by, but they knew of a medical situation in which I found myself, and at this time, the pressure of waiting for a kidney transplant was no further ado. I took the first insulin bottle, drew back on a syringe as far as it'd go, and took in as much insulin as possible. I remember lying on my back on the pull-out bed in my upstairs bedroom in my parents' house, contemplating: do I inject to my thigh, my arm? Does it really matter? After, there's nothing. My choice was my thigh; it was like holding a dart, getting ready to hit that target. I remember drawing back, going forward. Pulling back, going forward, "Stop being a pussy," I kept telling myself. If you're really serious about doing this, then just do it. Then bam, I felt the quick pinch of the syringe pierce my skin. The only thing left to do was expel the plunger, releasing this insulin, this toxic number of life-ending pharmaceuticals. Looking at the size of the syringe and how much insulin it contained, I knew it probably would not be enough to put me down for the final count. I didn't want to wind up in another medical situation or coma only to go through more rehabs and continue life even worse. Once again, I put a syringe back into the vial, drew back on it, and filled yet another syringe. I kept doing this until that vial was empty. Although the vial was empty, my body was filled with this metabolic drug. Being very familiar with insulin and its impact and how long it would take to go into effect, I knew I had a little time, so I began to sip on this nighttime cough medicine.

123

Maybe I would just drift off before the insulin kicked in; whatever attack, this would work.

You see, the effect of quick-acting insulin is roughly 30 minutes; at this point, I really didn't care because by then, I'd probably be unconscious, unable to communicate, unable to cry. Slowly, I began to feel the impact of the insulin. I shook a little. I began to sweat, and I was feeling weaker. I couldn't distinguish where it was coming from, the insulin or the cough medicine. But at this point, it didn't matter; it was working.

After twenty minutes, I found myself still awake, breathing, and conscious to the point where I was starting to drift out of it. The lights from the ceiling brightened, my eyes cracked open, and the window blew in some cool air, so I realized I still was here and still had some life. During these twenty minutes, I felt the emotions kicking as well. I began to cry. My mind was overloaded. I realized what I had just done and even questioned if I should have done it. Maybe I was not ready or just made a big mistake, but it was too late to take back what I'd already done. I needed to make a call, but to whom?

Ironically, the first people I thought about were my ex-wife TJ and my children; no way in hell would I call a child and explain to them that their father had just attempted to take his life and remove himself from this earth, making them fatherless. I dialed the phone quickly on the other end. What was the answer? "Hello."

It was TJ. She sounded like someone who maybe had been sleeping, but I needed to inform her what I had done; I didn't ask her to make any calls. I didn't ask her for help, but I confessed to her, "I did it; it's over. I just took a bottle of insulin. This is the last you'll hear from me," and I hung up the phone. Within fifteen minutes, there was a knock. "What should I say to him?" There was a rumble at my front door; I was too numb to get up and answer it. At this point, I couldn't even communicate. I remembered hearing a voice call out, "Mike, Mike, it's me. It's John, John C."

When I heard this, I wondered who Mike was and why he was calling out? I could hear footsteps, or feet, coming rapidly up the steps; an officer entered my room. I knew enough to let this officer know I was not Mike but Chris. Mike is my brother. The officer looked familiar; I'd just seen him in the past. I was actually friends with his nephew.

He had no further questions. It was obvious: a needle, insulin, a syringe, cough medicine, and I was pretty much out of it. He picked up his radio and called 911; five minutes, sirens were sounding and pulling up in front of my parents' house. By this time, at least eight adults filled my small 11 x 17 bedroom. Anyone from a paramedic to the fireman, questions were being thrown around. The wrong comments were being made. It was too much for me to comprehend then, but I knew they were doing their best to get me back on my feet, or should I say, back to life.

After some of these officers' assistance, I saw one remarking, "Chris, you realize when you take your insulin, you need to eat." I thought to myself, this guy is not really bright. Does he realize what I've just done? A paramedic on hand alerted his partner to get juice from the refrigerator. I was still awake enough to ingest something sweet, but at the same time, I was being administered glucagon. The paramedic remarked that the insulin was eating up whatever sugar was being put into his body. We needed to keep giving him more sugar. They start an IV drip of dextrose. They continued to give me juice and prepared to get me to the nearest medical facility.

That's how they usually handle things; wherever the nearest hospital is where they take their patients, one officer said, I guess we're headed for Lawrence. The paramedic responded, "No, not for this one; we're going to White Plains." You see, the reason for going to White Plains was not that it was a better hospital, but it was the fact that it was not only a medical situation; it was a suicidal situation. White Plains was able to handle patients with mental issues, which would be my destination.

Living in a small town, I knew almost everybody, and word would travel quickly, publicizing the matter at hand that night and somewhat announcing what I did. They were unaware of what I was dealing with; I'd managed to keep it in for years. I remember my parents were no longer local, and my brother was the closest person to me.

I remember finally arriving by ambulance at White Plains Hospital; I don't remember seeing him, but I knew his voice. My cousin Anthony, a family attorney, joined my brother's presence. I was wheeled through a small corridor and placed in a room as a nurse continually worked on me. I remember being soaking wet and asking the nurse if I could get something dry; she asked me, "did you pee yourself?" I explained: "No, I'm sweating and shaking and cold." Obviously, these were the adverse effects of the insulin still doing its work.

I lay alone under the nurse's watch, seeing as I was now considered harmful to myself. Seeing my condition, my sense of time was all over the place. I didn't know if it was night or day. Or what day of the week. I just knew I was back in the hospital again; my parents were the first set of people to visit. They had made it home from Florida. They were strong and calm, but you could see the fear, the questions, and the concern on their faces. The first question obviously was how I felt, and they did not ask what I did; they just wanted to know about my well-being.

Then my mother stopped, hesitated, before she asked and let it out: "Christopher. I have one question: how could you do this to those children?" At that point, I could feel myself well up in tears. I didn't have an honest answer, but I knew that wouldn't matter. Mind over matter came into effect; my mind was winning the battle, and the only thing I thought about was me.

When the doctor returned, my state of mind was still the same, and my first question to him was: when can I get out of here? As if to laugh, the doctor quickly responded: "Christopher, you're not going anywhere. You see, you tried to kill yourself." I thought to myself: "No shit." I didn't register the consequences of a failed attempt at suicide, but I did know I did not like his bedside manner.

The doctor also assured me that Columbia would be notified. It didn't take much for me to figure out that when he referred to Columbia, he meant the transplant team, which was in charge of notifying me when organ donors became available. Now it registered I had fucked up; I'd never see a transplant, especially if I was this much of a risk. No medical facility would be willing to take that chance or put in that much time for someone who was not medically sound and not responsible enough to care for themselves, let alone a newly transplanted organ from this point.

I do remember having to actually speak with a psychiatrist. He was nice. He asked normal questions, and I was comfortable with his answers. From this point forward, I still, to this day, cannot recall really what had transpired after being at White Plains Medical. What happened to me? What happened to that little chunk of life? Where did it go? OK, one thing I did know was I would be hearing from my ex-wife; sure enough, within the next couple of days, she definitely had some feedback for me. Her concern was our children. I needed to explain to them just what I did and why I did it. What was the reason? This would probably be one of the most difficult things I had to address in telling your child I basically did not want to live. How would they feel? Does Dad not love us anymore? Is he doing this to get away from us? Did we do something?

I could not be in their heads, but I needed to straighten things out for them. I needed to give them peace of mind. It took me a bit to get up my courage, but I owed that to them. I knew I could not be a coward and try to escape from this easily. That would be the easy thing to do, just avoiding them, but they're my children, and I love them. They need to be mentally sound. I don't need to fuck their minds up as well.

I sat down with both of my children. It was hard, but I opened up. I cried at times, but I let them know what I did. I listened quietly. I really didn't ask questions. I did have one comment, and the comment came from my daughter. She said, "It's OK; we knew this would happen. You were not happy; you didn't smile anymore. It was only a matter of time." I had no answers for her, only more tears. I thought I could reply, but that wouldn't be the right thing to do. What was I supposed to say? "Why didn't you tell me that?" You know it wasn't their responsibility. I remember repeatedly saying, "I'm so sorry, I'm so sorry." But at this point, whatever damage was done, I couldn't take back what I had done but only move forward.

I am their father. I'm supposed to be the one looking over them. At that point, the only thing I could think of was holding them tightly, telling them I loved them and was there for them. I wasn't going anywhere and would always look out for them.

CHAPTER 23: BACK IN THE GAME

At 125 pounds, soaking wet, I was half the person I used to be: my face sunken in, my clothes hanging off, and no muscle mass whatsoever. It was time to start over. I need to get back to the body I used to have, the athletic build, the 9% body fat. To lift 200 pounds-plus and have the stamina to get through a one-hour workout. Would this be possible? Remember, I was the type to rush things. I want things now, and I want things today, but to put on 30 pounds of muscle mass... it wasn't going to happen. Enter a new friend: Deca, Winnie, and Anabol. Yep, you guessed it: all names of anabolic steroids. I'd heard about them. I'd seen them; guys in the locker room used them, and access was fairly easy. All you needed was a little bit of money. I did all the reading on how to get steroids into your system. There was oral, and then there was your injectable; for the most part, oral was a little less effective than the injectable, so that was the route I would choose. After all, I was a pro at injecting; being a diabetic for 30+ years, needles pose no harm to me.

"It's never too late to be what you might have been." - George Elliott.

Needless to say, an insulin needle and a steroid needle were far from the same deal, for insulin injection was possibly a ½-inch in length and its gauge very thin; on the other end, your steroids syringe, or hypodermic, was about an inch and a half in length, real thick. The difference is now, you're pushing through something oil-based, not water-based. As I further researched some of these anabolic steroids or hormones, I learned how they did it and what side effects could be possible. Let's see, loss of hair... I'm bald. Acne... well, I can pop a pimple. Aggression, I isolate myself, so I won't get pissed at anybody; and last, impotence. As sad as it is, I laughed really hard at this one; ever since I was 24 years of age, I have dealt with ED (erectile dysfunction) and taking medication for me to sexually perform.

I saw four side effects of those mentioned--four of them I've already experienced or still experienced. I had nothing to lose. The problem was: who do I approach to get these? Should I ask around the gym? Should I Google it? Well, sure enough, the answer came from the gym. A friend of mine has been ordering and using some of these muscle advantages for quite some time now and had some connections. So, let's do this: go through him, give it a shot, and see how it goes the first go-round. I paid what was suggested, and I had what I needed within two weeks. I had never injected a needle in my ass before, but I can tell you it was not similar to an insulin injection; given that the steroid injection had to be done in either your thigh, shoulder, or buttocks, most seem to prefer their ass. The only thing I could tell you: it was like taking a carpenter's hammer and driving a nail into the uppermost part of your ass muscle. Your muscle spasms and burns for just a few seconds but then dissipates. Was that it?

Do it all over in one single injection within another week. The day after I had taken the injection, I slowly started to walk with a limp. My friend had explained that the oils being absorbed by your body created cramping or the pain I felt in the rear. I guess my first question was: is the pain worth it? Was

I going to see results again? Being young, although I was impatient, I didn't see results quickly but did slowly and gradually. My body was returning slowly: muscles rounded out, calves got like softballs, biceps like cannon balls, and shoulders wider than a door entry. Of course, I'm exaggerating a bit, but overall, I did put on some serious muscle mass; in no time, I went from 125 pounds to about 153 pounds. I looked great; I felt great everything on the outside was working and looking promising. However, I was still living with what was going on inside; again, my mind was still not working properly, and with the addition of the steroids, it was probably even worse. To me, the development of muscles outweighed the risks. I continued to take these muscle-building supplements for quite some time-- probably over a year, often letting my body rest a little, then going back on. It seemed to be a successful method and a proven method; I got stronger, and I got bigger. I looked good; I was getting attention; you see, I had always loved the comic book scene and admired the super heroic bodies that enhanced the pages of the multiple comic books you could find at your local candy store. I wanted to be superhuman, untouchable, and indestructible, but the one battle I did forget was the one I was losing with my diabetes.

"Whoever holds the hammer, if he is worthy, shall possess the power of Thor." -Stan Lee.

As I mentioned, I had already had all the complications associated with using steroids, except the acne, which I slowly noticed was forming on my back. That was quick to cure. Each time I came off the muscle-building products, which most bodybuilders call a cycle, I did seem to lose a little bit of size and strength; but it was still worth what I was gaining. And to me, the outcome outweighed the risks, much like most of the progress I have made in my life, whether physical or mental.

There is always one step forward, two steps back, and this follows the same suit. After utilizing Deca-Durobolan, I slowly began to get headaches. I couldn't tell why I was getting headaches; maybe I was dehydrated, the amount of weight I was lifting, the pressure of exerting myself to such an extreme. Eventually, it turned out what the reason was: my blood pressure, which had originally been normal, had begun to rise so high that the Doctor put me on medication. The last thing I want to hear as a diabetic who has been taking medicine his whole life is that another component to my medical equation would be added. The doctors prescribed Metoprolol to help control my blood pressure and bring it down. Could I actually take this Metoprolol at the same time as the steroids? What does Metoprolol do to combat high blood pressure while using steroids?

Even though I was still introducing something into my system, did I want to take that chance? Did I want to risk another complication outside of the ones mentioned earlier? This was probably one of the few times my mind was functioning properly. I quickly decided to stop the utilization of this anabolic steroid, and I will be honest with you, mainly because of the money situation. The products were expensive, and hard to come up with cash to buy them; that being said, I also started to realize the importance of my blood pressure. I didn't want to risk having a stroke or a heart attack; that just wasn't worth it. As I said earlier, I would always maintain some of the muscle I had previously gained. At this point, I had somewhat of a structure that I could build off, continue to grow, and hopefully make some progress.

I spent days, nights, mornings, wherever I could get a workout in--even at home, utilizing my dumbbells and bench. I was still seeing the results. I was a good eater. I was interested in nutrition and followed good food guidelines by combining both. I managed to stay lean and carry a lot of muscle on my five-foot-six figure. Finally, I was somewhat happy with myself again; I would love to be a little bigger, leaner, and tighter. But in this case, the risks did not outweigh the reward.

An additional reason, which I previously mentioned as a complication, started to surface: mood swings. My head was already not screwed on tight, and I didn't need any other sways. In my thinking, I began to get a little short on matters; my attention span was less focused, and at times, I just felt like I wanted to explode. Sometimes the explosion felt like it would be so big and powerful. The pen and pad were not the right choices to vent. I felt more like punching a wall or throwing a dumbbell. I didn't know how to get around this.

Should I go out for a run, exercise? Luckily enough, the only punishment I did put out was a punishment to myself. I didn't physically cause harm; I began to look at myself as worthless, useless. I wanted to isolate myself again; I wanted to be alone. I didn't want to be part of anything other than what I thought about, how I felt, and how I was going to get through a day?

Before injecting these steroids, I had already been through enough; I didn't need to add to it mentally. The regimen of steroids was slowly weaned off and eventually stopped. I was able to put a little bit of money back in my pocket and alleviate a little bit of stress, anxiety, and many mood swings.

Another positive thing that came out of this experience in life was that I became certified as a personal trainer, a lifestyle and weight management consultant. I even took it as far as becoming a life coach. After thinking more clearly, I figured I knew what I'd been through. How can I help people avoid these obstacles? What kind of suggestions can I give? Will they be willing to take them?

CHAPTER 24: ROTOR-ROUTER

The constant visitation to visit my friends (my medical friends) continued. Seeking out various specialists, whether it be dealing with Diabetic Neuropathy, Erectile Dysfunction, or even my newly diagnosed high blood pressure. By this point, my kidneys were getting worse, and it was time to start looking for donors and adding my name to the National Donors list. I wasn't quite ready for a transplant yet, and my kidney function wasn't quite low enough for dialysis, so I still had some time, which was quickly diminishing. Before this happened, there would be a series of medical work-ups like health history, urine, blood samples, blood typing, and seeing a staff psychiatrist, who determined I was mentally fit and had the support I would need during this process. Luckily enough, when it came to sitting with NYP financial team, the best piece of news I had received in a long time was that my insurance would cover the procedure and the abundance of pharmaceuticals I'd be ingesting after the surgery. Of course, this was all short-lived; when a stress test turned up, I had a major blockage to the main artery of my heart. Although I had no clue that this would have turned up in a scan, I must admit I was feeling some of the symptoms for quite some time; but I took it as needing more cardio at the gym. After all, I was at this time (pre-surgery) probably 5 foot 6, around 163 pounds, and about 7% body fat, so I wasn't convinced it was a physical issue. Going upstairs, steep hills, or maybe trying to lift a heavy load became a task with labored breathing and sometimes even collapsing; so that being said, what was on deck next was treating this diagnosis and having it done ASAP, so I could be registered as a possible donor recipient with ENOS (National Kidney Donor Registry).

ASAP was an understatement: within the next 3 days, I found myself lying on my back, semi-exposed, where my cardiologist proceeded to push a catheter into my groin, eventually reaching the clogged artery. I was lying there cold, somewhat sedated, but I could feel the catheter make its way through my body. The procedure didn't exhibit any pain but rather an odd, unfamiliar feel of something foreign passing through my body. The procedure was successful, and I could leave the hospital that day under supervision. Throughout this timeline of a medical mishap, this experience was a real eye-opener or, should I say, literally, the unexpected. Again, the common question arose, did risk outweigh the reward. Was it the steroids that contributed to a newly placed stent in my chest? One thing I did know, the poor control over my Diabetes for so many years was definitely a factor.

CHAPTER 25: MARIA

It's March 31, 2020, and the night's ending. I'm on the phone with a new girlfriend right now. She's my focus; she's all I can think about, despite Maria being so far from where I lived--actually, Jersey. I still was overjoyed at this opportunity of forming a relationship. Maria and I had met on a dating app; we started off by saying, and I quote, so close yet so far; and what I meant by that was everything we had talked about, everything we'd written in our profiles, we had liked about each other just clicked; however, the distance between us meeting, plus travel time, was just so far. I would often explain: you know, I do travel down to Jersey in the summers. I do go down there with my family. Nothing says I can't come down to visit. We can walk the boardwalk.

Maria was ecstatic about this. She would've loved to meet, but there wasn't enough time. Was that what we really wanted? Sometimes seeing somebody for the first time and having something could be worse; how do you pull away from that someone? Maybe this wasn't such a good idea.

All I knew was I enjoyed talking to Maria. She listened, and I listened. We each gave each other positive feedback; it was laughs. There were times we cried; I think we shared every emotion the mind is capable of. Things began to come together with Maria and me, which were happening quickly. We were both destined to travel, whether one hour or two hours, just to meet up, to actually see each other in person, and touch each other's skin, feel each other's hair--not mine, of course, because

I'm bald; but you know what I mean. Just get to know the real person.

When I spoke to Maria, I felt like the average guy. There was nothing wrong with me. I wasn't broken. She was a girl showing interest in me, and even more so, she wanted to meet me. I had been married for 17 years; I had two beautiful children and was still newly divorced. Not only was I finally feeling independence, but I was feeling acceptance; somebody wanted to get to know me, and I wanted to get to know somebody else. Believe me, in the back of my mind, which always moved quicker than my mouth, I was thinking, what if... yeah, you guessed it: What if this relationship worked out? What if there was some form of intimacy with this woman I had just met? How would I introduce my issues-- my man-problems? I said, "Slow down, Chris, she's two hours away. This is probably not going to happen. Let's worry about it then."

My phone rang no sooner than I calmed down and took my mind off that subject. Somebody was trying to get through on the other line. I told Maria I needed to excuse myself to check who it was. It was a familiar number. It had a 212-area code. I knew 212 was New York City, and the only person or place I knew that would be calling this early in the morning would be New York Presbyterian. As I clicked over to the second line, I heard a woman's soft voice state: "Is this Christopher Romano?" I answered yes; she explained that she was one of the coordinators at New York Presbyterian and that they had found a donor, a match.

She was a match for a kidney and a pancreas; they continued to explain who the woman was, why she died, and whether I would be willing to accept this donation? The formality is that some donors may have had diseases like hepatitis or AIDS. They might have been drug users, but ultimately all the organs were tested safely for transplant. A nurse strongly suggested it because this donor was a complete match. I was not necessarily the recipient; a normal protocol would be the call I received followed by an additional call. If I were the recipient, she told me to sit back, relax, get a good night's sleep, and wait. At that point, I thought to myself: is she crazy? Seeing what she just told me, how do I relax? How do I sleep? The only thing I could say was: I understand. I do accept, and I will wait for your call. And that was not to be very optimistic.

I clicked back to Maria and explained where the call came from. Maria broke into tears as I tried to pacify the situation and explain how it worked; in doing so, twenty minutes had passed, and the phone rang again.

"Is this Christopher Romano?"

"Yes, it is Christopher."

"We have a match; the match is yours. We need you here by 4:30 a.m."

Now my heart sank, my body shook, and I didn't even know what to say, holding everything back in a broken tone. I asked the nurse: what do I do next? As calmly as possible, the nurse explained I needed to be at the New York Presbyterian emergency room by 4:30 a.m. and pack a bag.

That was all she needed to tell me. After getting off the phone with the nurse, I clicked back again to Maria. I explained where my situation stood and what I needed to do. Maria's constant question was: what should I do? What should I do? At that point, I felt extremely bad for Maria; she was more than two hours away. She can't be here, but she wants to be here. She's asking me what she can do. What do I tell her?

I managed to calm Maria down and explain to her: "Here is my mother's number. Utilize it whenever and wherever you want, but I will be out of contact from 4:30 a.m. onward tomorrow morning. Everything will be all right, just say a prayer, and what's in the cards is in the cards. We will get through this; we'll get through it together." I remember Maria saying that she needed to see me. She needed to see me so bad; she needed to be with me; this coming from a girl whom I had never met before—only texting and phone calls-- so I repeated: "Here is my mom's number; I will let her know who you are and why you're calling."

After ending my conversation with Maria, it was time to pack a bag, but I forgot one thing: I still didn't tell my parents. They were asleep in the next room. Quickly I ran and explained the situation, as if we had to leave within the next five minutes, not much like on TV when you see somebody receiving a donation. Do you have to immediately fly to Oregon or somewhere, get there within the next 10 minutes, and have it put into somebody's chest or body? It's slightly more relaxed than that, but I needed to get there ASAP.

4 a.m. was nearing, and we were halfway down to the New York Presbyterian Medical Center, where we were checking in. It was quiet; the hospital was dark. It was pretty much motionless at the time. Very sad: Mom, Dad, and myself in a waiting room with just a receptionist; she took down all the information—insurance and so forth—and pulled up my charts. The only thing left to do was wait for the organs. I slowly gathered more information from the receptionist in preparation. They would begin to prepare me at 4:30 a.m., and the surgery would not actually begin until 8:30 a.m. You see, the organs I received were being flown in from Wisconsin.

Before I knew it, a four-hour distance between 4 a.m. and 8 a.m. had passed. I was primed and ready, nightgown on, laid out in bed. IVs hooked up; anesthesia ready to go. The only thing we were waiting for was the final preparation of the organs. As I slowly was wheeled down to the OR, the last thing I remember hearing was my mother saying: "It's been a long time, Christopher. Now is your time."

As I entered the ER, it was a spotless, stainless steel and white room. The first person I passed was the actual surgeon. She introduced herself. "You may already know, but I wanted to make sure we were on the same page," she lightheartedly said. "Christopher, would you like to see your organs?" Which I thought was a joke, but it wasn't. They showed me the two organs that would slowly be put into my body, giving me life again. Like most procedures or operations, lights are out once you're under the gun or the anesthesia; nothing is evident, and you no longer exist. Your body is no longer with you; ironically, you wake up. Where am I? What happened? Why am I here?

And ironically, after three hours in recovery, those questions were answered:

"Christopher, the transplant was successful. You're in recovery."

Little did I know, I had been in surgery for seven hours? The next stop was the intensive care unit; there were only a limited number of people who could visit at this time; I couldn't even tell you who visited. I heard voices but couldn't comprehend them. I was still in a daze. After several more hours, I was awake and could associate faces with names. I spit out a couple of sentences and even smiled; most of my family had been present--a cousin or two and my daughter, from what I could make out. I understood why my son Jordan had not come because he was an emotional boy, much like me: somewhat sheltered and sometimes unable to handle seeing loved ones in certain situations like mine, but he was with me in my heart. After the crowds had cleared, and my parents were still left behind, my mother left me a brief message: Maria called; she wanted to know how you were doing?

Regardless of the state of mind that I was in, the name Maria was as clear as day, like I had just gotten off the phone with her. My mother explained she was doing everything possible to get to the hospital. She needed to see me and be there as soon as possible. I understood what my mother said; I didn't fully comprehend everything. Needless to say, the next day Maria arrived. Not only did Maria travel a distance, but she also traveled to see a man she had just met-- a new man--and battled through traveling during a Covid epidemic. I truly felt this was the woman. This was my partner, my soulmate. The woman I was meant to be with; after several days in the hospital, again, there was another return home. We'd been through this before: do a little battle in the hospital, survive, and come home for recovery. I was used to the drill; amazingly enough, Maria would return during this recovery time. She'd visit. Our limited time together was very therapeutic, almost healing; again, I felt alive and independent but not alone. I had somebody to listen to and communicate with as my recovery continued. I kept in contact with Maria.

Unfortunately, Covid continued to get worse. Our ability to travel across the bridge was being prevented. Governor Cuomo was setting limitations on everything; our contact was limited to texts, FaceTime, and phone calls, nothing more than voices and words, understandably, and we cannot choose our fate. We can have a lot to do with it, but something more powerful was in the cards. In this case, the cards I was dealt and Maria's cards did not have us in the future; amicably, we had to say goodbye between the distance and Covid.

We were actually losing it. Mentally we were unable to function; we missed each other. We wanted to be with each other, but if it wasn't possible, we needed to stop this torture. It was like somebody teasing another, like holding or dangling something before my face, something you couldn't grab hold of.

Outside of my relationship with my ex-wife, Maria was my very first relationship. She is still near and dear to my heart; although we don't keep in contact, losing Maria was like losing a year of therapy. I slowly started to slip back again, feeling isolated, broken, depressed, and unwanted; all the demons were beginning to resurface.

How would I handle this? I'm really not ready for it. How can I deal with or get all this out? Who can I speak with? The only thing I ever knew to do when these problems resurfaced was reaching for a pen and pad, dig deep into my soul, and express myself by writing poetry. Just how I felt, just what I needed to do, if I could do it, or just something positive... something, when reading that, would be soft, gentle, and pleasing to the ear. Despite parting with Maria, I had sent her a framed poem I had written when we first met. Maria was very guarded, and I felt I needed to get through; she built a wall. A guard; she wouldn't let just anyone in. She had been through some troubled relationships. This was my attempt at getting through:

'I need to break down her wall and move in closer, remove her pain, and replace it. With my love. Although I already know why this wall exists, I need to listen, hear them again, and better understand why she has built these walls so high. Our relationship will only grow stronger; as soulmates as we slowly break down each other's walls, pull each other from isolation, and fight to understand each laid brick in that wall. Emphasize that, true, a wall may fend off the pain and disappointment, keeping out the unfaithful and so-called friends. But at the same time, it prevents those who care, love, and dream from sharing what life is meant to be, the respect, passion, and desire to become one. Standing side-by-side, rid our lives of the many bricks and instead show her, not tell her, how I would attempt to climb that wall to be with her, physically and mentally. We need to replace that wall with something higher, a mural painted alongside the tallest skyscraper, not to climb but admire, letting everyone know we are who we are; this is what we stand for and mean to each other. I need to demonstrate there comes a time to turn the page, not close the book, read her emotion, and her read mine. Be able to re-tell this story with a new beginning, a new chapter with no ending. This is not a fairytale but a biography of our love, life, and happiness. I must share that she is not lost but still loved and that even the most broken of hearts can still beat again. I need to establish and ensure the trust we have together and heal the wound, mend the scars, not to be forgotten because they made us who we are, instead burying them deep, not to be re-awoken again. Show her that thick skin and isolation are not the answer. I will show her another side of life through love and laughter, the kind of love that leaves no questions to be asked and that forgives and heals. I will replace those bricks with windows within those walls she has built, giving insight and promise and, if not enough, demonstrating the love and determination to climb, knock them down, conquer, and survive. I will ask her to look into my eyes, read my soul, and show her I was chosen; I was the voice that called out to her in a dream. I am; we are a reality, side by side, we go to war, confident there's no wall high enough to keep us apart, but just enough to keep us within."

CHAPTER 26: DO YOU BELIEVE IN ANGELS?

This book would not be complete without the acknowledgment of my one angel, who came and blessed the world I occupy. This individual sacrificed her life to give life to another. For purposes of this book, and out of respect for her family's privacy, I will call her by her first name only, Rebecca.

Rebecca came to me through two organs, a pancreas and a kidney. She now lives on within me in my heart and soul... There are not enough words or chapters in this book to understand my gratitude. There will come a day when you and I, Rebecca, will finally be introduced; this time, on your territory, high above the sky where the angels run, free from disease it does not exist, where people live every day like it's their last day, where there is only peace and harmony. Show me the way, and I'll meet you there, beyond the pearly gates. 'Til that time, I will do my best to pay it forward to others, the less fortunate people who need somebody to talk to or just be heard. You see, I cried out to somebody, and you were the one to answer the call. It is only fair that I pay this favor forward in being an angel for the others out there. There is no way to think of this individual outside of living my life to the fullest. I tried to contact Rebecca's family; however, I've had no luck or response. Out of respect, I had left it alone and left it at peace; the only way I know of paying it forward is a tribute to this individual, who gave up so much for someone she didn't even know:

"I am a child who has been scarred deeply, as deep as the ocean. I choose not to be tempted to sip that magic potion. I refuse to let myself drown in the unforgiving ocean. I try to forget the sense of pain, yet impossible; it hits hard like the forceful rain. I run for cover and swallow my pride; I am scared and need to hide. Although vague, I seem to remember I am the optimist, the fighter. Give me the strength to make this load lighter. Please send her, dear god, and bring her to fruition, for I can no longer accept my current position. Oh dear lord, it's been some time; let us break bread and share the wine. I ask you for help with all the confusion because, dear lord, I am tired of losing. I have found someone who lives within, so please answer my prayer, for I do not sin. Does she have a name I want to share, but what's the difference--her life, too, maybe not so fair? This is a woman to which I have grown; from day one, I will promise never to leave alone. She is my will and power, oh dear lord, I think of her every waking hour. Dear lord, you have done it before: parted the seas and opened a door. Provide the path to be taken, my love, not to be mistaken. Give me the key that you hold and unlock the gate, after all, there is still time, and it's not too late. Pass through those gates; I will roam; a prayer has been answered. I am not alone. Much like your angels who bear the feather, oh dear lord, I pray, bring us together."

CHAPTER 27: THE COMEBACK TRAIL

Sometimes I am asked some of the strangest questions after the transplant, but I also understand people are inquisitive; on the other hand, curiosity kills the cat. Some people I cross are not hesitant to ask: do you feel any different, or has your personality changed after the surgery? Which is a bold and brave question. And often, I am puzzled or actually bothered by it. Despite that, I try and have some fun with it, although it's a serious subject of discussion. Despite feeling grateful, I sometimes feel like a woman trapped inside a man's body (and I don't mean like Bruce—sorry, Catelyn Jenner). This is not far from the truth because, living with diabetes and poor glucose control, I did experience several symptoms you might've heard from the female persuasion. I continue to have my fingers get swollen, and so are my ankles. I feel bloated, and I get violent mood swings every 20-30 days, and this might be what I am experiencing now. I also crave something sweet and then something salty. But the oddest feeling is when I look down at my boobs; I never remember them being there, but they're nice boobs. Then it registers it's not a joke, but after all I've been through, sometimes I just have to break up the tireless angst hiding behind a little humor. But in honesty, when looking down, the only thing I do see is the 6-inch scar, like that of a C-section, I'm left with, which now crosses my midsection--the badge of courage I now wear with respect and admiration for my donor, who gave her life to give to another. The only oddity is that I don't exhibit any of her personality, but she does live within me, and the only feelings that I feel are her emotions and love that I welcomed into my heart. Being forever grateful, I pay it forward to others, looking for someone to listen and understand, much of which is why I wrote this book.

It had been a short time since the completion of my double-transplant surgery. I was so grateful. I thought I would be experiencing life for what was meant to be a better quality of life shortly after being home, which at this time was under my parents' roof. I realized I was feeling a little uneasy with myself, not so secure in how I walked, talked, or just got out of bed in the morning. Something was up. I'm not sure what it was, but I knew I always felt dizzy and out of control, almost like my body parts were not functioning as they should have been. It was later diagnosed that I was experiencing extremely low blood pressure. When I mean low, my numbers read 60/40, sometimes even lower--the norm having to be 120/80. The doctor suggested eating saltier foods to raise my blood pressure. I was getting up slowly before I got out of bed.., even more importantly, after a bowel movement. Still, most importantly, I stressed that I needed to intake plenty of fluids. At the same time, at home and integrating these suggested things to help accommodate the low blood pressure, I slowly began to experience lightheadedness all the time; a series of falls was something familiar in my daily routine.

Whether falling down a flight of steps or just passing out while standing still, it seemed a habit forming. The time had come that I needed a walker or something to give me a little more security, something to help me stand, walk, get around unassisted... give me a little more confidence. I was more than open to it; I just needed to get used to it. During this period, in medical terms, I continued to experience low blood pressure, known as orthostatic blood pressure. There had to be some recourse other than a walker and an adjustment in the diet on how to fix the situation, but nothing has been brought to my attention. I finally found enough courage to go upstairs to downstairs, but not before falling down one flight of steps. I was OK. I was used to pain, and the neuropathy usually killed off most of it.

When I returned to my feet, I explained to my parents that I wanted to go outside. They were more than happy to accommodate me. Again I got a flashback; much like my childhood, I was being looked after by my parents. Yep, big brother. I knew they were concerned, but I still wanted my independence. I wanted to go out on my own. I wanted to walk on my own and use the bathroom on my own. I just wanted some sense of freedom.

We agreed we would walk around the blocks, maybe do a lap or two, all with the assistance of a walker. We did this for some time before I finally concluded; I wanted to be upfront and firm: "Mom, Dad, I'm doing this on my own." On that day, I made sure I had my trusty walker and cell phone and made my way around the block. I took some time, a few stops, and a little winded, but I did it. Yes, I did it, and I did it on my own: one lap today. Maybe another tomorrow. Progress.

Much of my life involved making progress: one step forward, two steps back. Any progress being made was taken away oh so quickly. Much of that was my fault because I always rushed to finish things. I wanted to meet my goals as if ready to be achieved the next day or within the next hour; I was impatient. I just wanted to feel better again; I wanted quality of life. I wanted to function on my own. I wanted to be my own person, but my pressure continued to remain low, and at this point, we finally realized medication was needed.

I began taking two types of medication meant to help raise my blood pressure; initially, it was great. It felt like it was on the right track. I could get up a little easier, stand a little longer, and function better, but it was temporary, much like any progress. The pills did not work anymore. Still under the aid of a walker, I continued to do my laps around the block, get a little stronger, get a little more flexible, and keep those muscles pumped and limber. As progress was made in this area, blood pressure and something else seemed relevant. I was having multiple bowel movements, repeatedly—yesterday, throughout the night, throughout the day, as if a baby needing a diaper change. I could not figure out just what was doing this. My mother and I tried to look at what I eat each day... could it be dairy? Could it be fiber? What could be doing this? What would make this happen? We did things like eliminating or adding different things, always managing to keep hydrated. None of this seemed to be enough. When it came to the point that I began to actually no longer have complete control over my movements, it had to be addressed.

The doctors at New York Presbyterian suggested I have a stool sample done and be tested for any viral infection or other outside entity trying to attack my new organs. That was easier said than done: I'd been going like rapid-fire, like kids used to say: The Hershey squirts. Things were coming out of the backside that I couldn't even explain and were coming fast. I ensured the next time I had a movement, a sample was ready to go. At this point, they could not diagnose anything about the sample. There was no viral infection. They said nothing at the time existed, maybe due to the surgery. I got a small infection and needed to heal over time; boy, were they wrong. Within the next day or two, I found myself hospitalized at White Plains Hospital in New York; not only was I at the hospital, I found they were admitting me.

During my admittance at the hospital, again, I found myself a prisoner, much like at Cornell--the difference being the nurses were a lot nicer and accommodating. I also knew under the care of White Plains, they would control my newly transplanted organs and my blood sugar, blood pressure, and so forth. As the days went by, I continued to have to use, at this point, a commode because nurses would not allow me to get up from my bed due to the low blood pressure and fainting, which I can understand for insurance purposes. Bowel movements were still coming rapidly. At this point, anything solid was now liquid coming out like a running faucet. It seemed like I never got off the commode. I think, at times, I might've even dozed off.

I actually felt bad for some of the nurses because the commode had to be changed so readily that it seemed like they never left the room; it finally took one nurse on a particular night to realize that this was not normal. She told me she was taking a sample and sending it to the lab. It took the labs at White Plains and the growth of this virus to finally be diagnosed after four days. Now keep in mind, during those four days, I still had multiple movements and a high loss of fluids from my body constantly hooked to an IV, and I was limited to where I could walk or move around my room. I would get as far as the commode each day, and that was it. The nurses even set the alarm on my bed; if my feet touched the ground creating a change in the weight distribution of my bed, something would sound in their office.

The bottom line was I was really never in my bed. I had spent so much time on this commode rather than getting up. I would just sit there, turn on the T.V. and let things run. Just let things fly out of my ass after the virus had grown for roughly four days. Yep, you got it: after four days of constant bowel movements, they determined I had C-Diff, a G.I. virus that could be treated. Their answer was initially, "We were unaware of the virus, so we did not know how to treat it. Now that we know what it is, we know how to follow up immediately."

I was hooked up to another IV. Another tube filled with a wonder drug. I called them wonder drugs because I often wondered if they worked, not because they're wonderful or if they prevent or cure the problem. The name of the antibiotic being introduced to my system was called Vancomycin.

Slowly but surely, symptoms began to subside. I still utilized the commode and had frequent bowel movements, but it definitely lessened. After a total of nine days in White Plains Hospital, it was finally determined that I could hold down enough fluids and hold off enough bowel movements to return home and try and function in my normal everyday life. I hate to use the word "normal" because nothing seemed normal to me. It was always a challenge. Doctors coined me as the 1% Patient. It meant that I was the 1% case where my illness was difficult to diagnose. I never presented just one problem but an abundance all at the same time. I wasn't textbook; they couldn't flip through some chapter of a medical dictionary, see what something was called, see what the remedy said, then go about it and fix it. I was the one who kept the physicians' wheels turning and had to be collaborative with other specialists, not just one doctor but a team of doctors, to try and come to a positive conclusion. And I can honestly say I still wasn't ecstatic at the fact that I was not completely cured, but what I was excited about was that I was being released, released back to a safe place--my home.

Sure, I might still be under the watch of big brother, meaning my parents, but it wasn't under the control of a medical physician or his colleagues, where I felt treated once again like a human specimen. Being home was good. It was nice to sleep in my bed and use my bathroom. I continued to take my walks slowly for a little bit longer. On top of this, I still had to readily fit in an appointment to have bloodwork done every week with a test to see that my organs were functioning properly. This became a routine where I'd walk myself out to the car, using my walker, and jump in the backseat, off to Tarrytown, where a local lab would draw my blood. Everybody there knew me like I was their best friend. It felt good to talk with some people I knew, see what they did the past weekend, and whatnot. I began to socialize again, where I knew faces, names, and things about these people; they knew things about me. It was a commonplace, another place, a safe place having blood done every week, the typical for a post-transplant patient. Once numbers, meaning blood values, started to hit their landmarks, numbers were where they should be, my appointments would be less frequent. Meaning my blood work would be reduced.

By this point, my doctor extended my blood work from going every week to two weeks, meaning two times a month. I had no problem with this. It was nice for it to be stretched out. I still enjoyed seeing my friends over in Tarrytown, and it was always a good feeling to see my blood values in check, meaning my organs were still functioning properly.

We still had to address one situation still not under control the orthostatic blood pressure. We had tried everything possible, including medication, to regulate these numbers; there was still no resolution. Something needed to be done before I wound up hurt or even dead falling down the steps. I would often laugh at that, but when you think about it, it is no joke when just fainting out of the blue. Who knows? If you hit your head, you may get a bruise, or worse, you may not wake up.

Day after day, I woke, took my time getting out of bed, and slowly shifted to a chair before I would get up to walk and slowly make my way over to my walker. See, the walker became a problem because I was living on the second floor and always needed to function, whereas the kitchen was downstairs on the first floor. I would take my time each morning, scooting down the steps on my backside. Yes, my ass shifting my way down 'til I got to the bottom. I waited a couple of seconds and then stood. We now had two walkers: one upstairs and one downstairs; it was like a nursing home, completely equipped for those unable to function and much-needed assistance.

I continued my routine the same way: get out of bed, go downstairs, eat, make my way back up, get cleaned up, and maybe go for a walk. Slowly, I did get stronger. Slowly my stomach got a little better, and miraculously, my blood pressure returned to where it should be. When I say the blood pressure was where it should be, I'm really saying it was high enough for me to function yet still low. More progress would be needed in terms of recuperation.

For now, I was living with my parents. I had enough assistance. The blood pressure was looking better, and I felt ready to return to work at this point in time. Outside of my control, something else was going on in the world, and that was what everybody, not just me, was dealing with Covid.

Covid hit this state like a storm. Nobody knew what it was or how to handle it. The only thing we did know was it was killing our people. It was strongly advised that I not return to work, for the building where I was employed was currently under construction, and there would be many construction workers and employees coming and going in and out of the facility daily. I could not risk any contamination, seeing as I was now immunocompromised; as a result, my place of employment agreed to set me up at home as a teleworker. The teleworker does precisely what they do in the office, except attend to the public. They do all their paperwork on the computer, answer phone calls, etc.

This is probably a dream to most: I get to work at home. I can get so much done at home, but little did I know when working from home that an employer can count every keystroke, every phone call,; monitor every document you put on the computer again. Big brothers were watching; once, I was set up from home, utilizing my own laptop; I got somewhat of a system where I'd wake up, eat something light, jump on the computer, and jump off at lunch. Jump back on after lunch and finish my day, seven hours in one room, five days a week... a prisoner again. You would think that the theme of my story is the prisoner; it just seemed like a new way of being this locked-up person, that boy in the bubble that I related to earlier as John Travolta. I knew this was temporary and would give after a while; boy was I mistaken. I think almost everybody was mistaken.

Covid continued to grow throughout our country. We didn't know how to handle it or have a cure. We didn't have something to prevent it. Scientists were looking for some method to this madness, as the continued reports came through on the news about the advances towards Covid cures and possibilities of injections, inoculations, etc. I listened intently. I think everybody did in my household. It was almost like we held a ceremony in the morning to listen to Governor Cuomo. Jumping ahead, I had probably been working at home for two years before I was first introduced to the Covid injection, and I was actually one of the first ones to receive it. (I was immuno-compromised.)

I was still given a choice to work from home. I was questioning the fact, unsure if I would like to make that attempt to come back. My employer was gracious in that they were not rushing me or asking me; they were just giving me an option. Now, you know me, my theory, and my outlook on life: I feel isolated. I feel like a prisoner. I want out. I want back.

I finally discussed it with my parents and decided: at the time, it would be June 1, two years at home had been long enough, and I had the vaccination. Initially, it seemed like June 1 was so far away, yet it snuck up on me. It was time to return. In the morning, I made my way to work: nothing had changed, the same commute, the same group of faces were at work, and the same work needed to be done. Just as if I hadn't left. By day four of my return, we received an announcement that four of our employees had contracted Covid. My initial instinct was: what do I do?

Ironically, even though my employers announced this, I was never approached or told to leave the site. However, employees on site within the last five days were instructed to go for Covid tests. I had no problem in doing that. I took it upon myself to approach my employer and say I'd be doing this alone and would not return until Covid was cleared. My employer totally understood the situation and just asked that I send a doctor's note in response to the test I would receive.

I needed to get to the doctor, get tested, and get home; lucky enough, my tests panned out to be negative, meaning there were no signs of Covid. It was quite some time before I made my second return to my employment. At this time, construction was still ongoing. People wore masks; at least most people wore masks. There were a select few. When not being watched, they felt the need to slide these fabric barriers down below their noses and their mouths, exposing any innocent bystander, only thinking of themselves and not what they may cause to others. The office environment progressed and got a little better in cleanliness, free of dust, germs, and fewer work orders, which meant fewer people passing through.

At the same time, our world was getting a little more advanced in technology and moving a little further in understanding Covid, what it was about, where it came from, how to prevent it, and possible treatments. I can't say that I didn't care. It was just that it was my makeup. I never really felt too concerned about my health and always looked out more for others, so going back to work a second time was inevitable. I was ready to do it. I took precautions, but I needed to be back out in reality.

"There are plenty of difficult obstacles in your life. Don't allow yourself to become one of them." - Ralph Marston...

CHAPTER 28: POP GOES THE WEASEL!!

I knew I was strong, and I'd been challenged before, but recovery after the transplants was nothing physically comparable to what I had ever experienced before. Under the watchful eyes of my gracious hosts at Hotel Romano, I continued to recover, ingesting pills daily. The pharmacy I had created in my bedroom housed as many as 15 bottles containing pills of brightly colored shapes, sizes, and odors. During the recovery phase, the doctor's methodology was to wean some of the pills in my arsenal as the risk of infection diminished. However, the risk of rejection would be lifelong, and my ammo was prescribed regularly to combat the rejection of the new organs. Much like my lab visits, I would slowly reduce the intake of most of my medication. The medications were all to be taken daily, not all at once, but throughout the day. I had a fancy pillbox marked "Monday through Sunday" filled for each time of the day. I would religiously pop open that pillbox, take my pills, and continue my day. As time progressed, meaning months, I started to wean from some of these medications... three months, six months, twelve. By the time I hit the 12-month, meaning my first year, I had probably dropped at least five bottles. I was excited about it but would be even more excited if there were no pills.

I understood I'd be taking pills for the rest of my life. Most importantly, anti-rejection pills are necessary so my organs wouldn't reject the transplant. Let's face it: somebody had to die to give life. In essence, I truly believe by accepting these organs, this person's life still lives throughout me, so I'm going to make the most of this and pay it forward, treat these organs right, and make them last. After a couple more months, most of the antibiotics fighting off my infections were removed from my cocktail of daily medications.

Left with only one particular medication called Tacrolimus; it is one of the drugs that will help my body reject any foreign antibodies and keep my organs working. That, too, was a crapshoot; initially, there were several types of anti-rejection drugs. However, in my case, as the 1%, each one had some kind of an adverse effect on my body--mostly my G.I. tract.

Faithfully, every other week I would sit in the backseat of my private Uber (aka Mom and Dad) and proceed down the W. Side Highway to New York City to have blood drawn. Luckily enough, I was quite vascular, an easy draw for the vampires ready to feed; the 9 vials of blood were easily accessible. With each day came repetition, like a scene from "Ground Hog's Day" starring Bill Murray, the alarm clock would sound off, and the cycle began, finding myself asking, "Haven't I done this before?" But then there would be a break in that chain, finding I was now dealing with another imbalance in my medical profile. A consistent pattern became noticeable in my blood draws, bringing concern for the possibility of rejection or injury to my new kidney. When elevated, the culprit, Creatinine levels (a chemical waste product removed entirely by the kidney), can create concern for infection, injury, or worse, rejection.

As a result, the doctor ordered an ultrasound and biopsy of the new kidney.

I was accustomed to ultrasounds and aware of the procedure, but a biopsy was foreign to me. The biopsy consisted of a needle inserted into my abdomen, similar to a pregnant woman with amniocentesis. Further explaining, I can relate (as explained in an earlier chapter) and sympathize with what they expect of mothers who choose to have the procedure out of concern for their unborn child. You may be scratching your head now, asking, "Aren't the kidneys located in the dorsal (back) part of the torso?" Sorry for all the medical terminology, but you must understand by this point in my life, I probably have more medical experience through my own medical challenges than a first-year med student. Not to say I was comparable to Dr. Oz, but I am well-versed in the field. So back to the question on the location of my new organ. The kidney is strategically placed in the frontal area of the torso, to the left of my belly button. Although not a member, but a supporter of the LGBTQ community, I was taking on my own form of transition. Genetically born a male, now part of a medical miracle (all kidding aside, still amazed by the transplantation procedure) as a result, my anatomical design, now different from the original but a hybrid version (some might say an upgrade or Limited Edition) primed and ready, the foreign citizen now naturalized to do its job from its new home and environment. The biopsy is a calculated procedure performed by the doctor utilizing another medical masterpiece; anticipating being placed under this apparatus, I pictured a contraption probably costing more than three homes in Beverly Hills. However, the device was handheld and made from plastic. Basically, a spring-loaded device called an Auto-Ject. This device is very similar to what was used by Doctor W when he inserted the needle and brought back the excitement and vigor of a teenage boy on prom night. In addition, an ultrasound would be utilized to mark the precise spot of the position of the needle where the term "guided" is associated regarding the depth and position of the needle. Once inserted, minute kidney fractions are extracted and examined for damage or risk of rejection. Being exposed to needles was quite familiar to me, more predominately being used when I struggled with Type I Diabetes, where insulin administration was required (if I had listened to what I just said, "required," reminding you of my ignorance in realizing the need for this drug and maintenance of the Diabetes as seen in an earlier chapter, I probably wouldn't be in this situation):

"Mistakes are always forgivable if one dares to admit them." –Bruce Lee.

I was pretty comfortable with going in for this procedure, except I needed to stay under observation for 3 to 4 hours at the hospital following the biopsy, again not my favorite place to unwind and celebrate happy hour. The time had come, and before I knew it, I was all set up at New York Presbyterian for the biopsy. Again, the procedure was a guided needle, so there was a small margin to have any complications. Flashback to an earlier chapter; remember, I am one percent prone to disaster. The doctor carefully placed the needle over my abdomen, and the countdown began, 321 click OK, that wasn't so bad. Only felt like somebody was driving a tiny nail into my stomach (sarcasm); the needle was thin, probably an inch long, and only went about 2cm deep. So, looking back at those expecting mothers, score, Chris zero mom's in waiting one, you definitely get the credit on this one. Anyway, at this point, I was feeling good about the situation. I've been dealt more pain before; can I handle two more times? 3-2-1 click! OK, one more to go, 3-2-1 click! I clutched the bed's side rails and cinched my butt cheeks so tight as if I would never allow another bowel movement to pass again; my back stiffened. I remained quiet, but my brain said, "What the fuck was that?" Almost immediately, I felt as if my abdomen exploded, my stomach on fire as if the pit of hell, and I am certain I saw the devil for a split second, exhibiting a small smirk, dressed in his blue scrubs.

I was dazed and confused, trying to snap out of this blindsided attack that overcame me, but unsuccessful; I couldn't figure out what was going on and was a bit disjointed; the one good thing was I was lying down and anchored. I felt faint, washed out, sweating profusely; you would have thought I just went 15 rounds with Ali or for the mothers out there, been in labor for way too long, just get this kid out, and that's what I prayed for, just get me out of this mess. In addition to the discomfort and pain, thinking to myself, if medical staff held up a chart with happy and sad faces asking me how I would rate the pain, I swear I would have utilized that needle on them. To keep me alert and now feeling lethargic, the lights began to dim, and the doctors continued to ask me questions. Meanwhile, I had no idea what I was saying, trying to communicate with hand gestures (no, not the one you are thinking) and using words, if you want to call it that, exiting my mouth as if I'm hungover from an all-night booze binge. This wasn't a glamorized episode of NYPD Blue, where the ever so attractive police officer, cut from G.Q. magazine, track down the perp. Followed by the would-be killer, now bleeding after being penetrated by the officer's bullet managing to spill his beans, having just enough time to tell the cop where the money is, who his accomplices are, and he's too young to die. This was surreal. It was happening and happening fast. Ironically, I wasn't concerned, almost relieved; maybe this was it. This time I might be down for the count. Did this cat finally exhaust life number 9? I had come so far mentally, and now the little voice was telling me just give in. Maybe it was the loss of blood or lack of oxygen to my brain thinking, "Snap out of this, you ungrateful prick" I didn't want to hear there were people worse off or you've come such a long way. I was tired of being in these situations. But there was no choice this time, and probably for the better, out of my control with medical staff behind the wheel and my designated drivers. Where is my Angel now?

The room filled quickly with a team of doctors surrounding my bed. I could not make out faces, but I heard a lot of commotion. What I did feel was somebody literally straddling me and not the type of straddling you'd welcome.

Finding both his hands right below my waistline to compress my abdomen downward to stop the internal bleeding. It seemed to work for the most part and was more uncomfortable than the biopsy, making me feel helpless and nauseous; this was only a temporary Band-Aid for the situation. The room was finally under control, and my stability was more evident. Before I knew it, I signed waivers, not for my life, but for blood transfusions, if I remember 2 to 3, and instantly became a hotel guest that night for observation. The number of times I occupied a hospital room, I should be considered a resident or at least have vested interest or cooperative ownership of one of their rooms. Turns out that with the last stick, or, should I say, hammering of the nail, my newly transplanted organ was grazed upon the puncture of my abdomen. The next few days, I was extremely sore, and I felt like I hired Arnold Schwarzenegger as my personal trainer; I didn't get the six-pack abs, but I did feel like I put in a valiant effort in trying to attain them. Sitting up was a bit of a task, and moving around overall. Still, seeing there was no parting of the "Red Sea," meaning there was no blood in my urine, and the last ultrasound presented a much happier kidney, I could escape the madness and return home. Drama such as what unfolded on that day is summed up beautifully by Eric Greitens, in that situations like I found mine provide for us to grow, adapt, withstand, and even overcome our most traumatic events in life, more importantly, realize we are all human, we cry, bleed and breathe the same air, we are not immortal, but all have our fate pre-determined.

"No one escapes pain, fear, and suffering. Yet from pain can come wisdom, from fear can come courage, from suffering can come strength - if we have the virtue of resilience".

Ironically, resilience has been an asset that, without it, I don't believe I could have survived or dodged the many bullets shot in my direction, navigating my unpredictable pathway in the search for solace.

CHAPTER 29: ON-LINE SHOPPING

Being divorced for three years and starting to feel somewhat up to par on the medical end, I finally persuaded myself to start making some changes. This time, things would be different; seeing the transplant had reversed nerve damage in a few parts of my body. The one that mattered most when entering this circle of newfound friends. I was ready to march again with the rest of the "Wooden" Soldiers; the piece of equipment that once was a pin cushion was back to form. So, I needed to finally come out from under that rock, or in my case, burst the bubble of isolation. To engage in a more social environment, I decided to do what most divorcees did: join online dating. Don't get me wrong: I wasn't the most comfortable with it, and I wasn't quite ready to swipe to the left or to the right (if you know what I mean), but I needed to be around company other than family and explore what was out there. With so many apps available, I decided to focus on just one, which was extremely user-friendly: create a profile, include some pics, and you are on the way to the promised land. I say this very lightly because my first perception of this site was that I was shopping out of a catalog of prospective friends, possible lovers, and, almost inevitably, stalkers and catfish.

'Now I know why I have always chosen to isolate and, as a teen, chose not to be involved in a relationship. By doing so, I am the only one who can hurt me, the only one who can disappoint me, and the only person to blame is me. My problem is I chose to listen to someone I see as special, and I chose to wear my heart on my sleeve and open up, exposing all my vulnerability. Unsure of why I haven't learned by now to just slow down and not get caught up in the emotions.

I will say, luckily enough, I only had one interaction with someone posing as an alter-ego. I could detect it quite quickly because her profile said African-American, her pics were of an Asian woman, and the age she claimed was 42 (let's give her the benefit of the doubt), but she looked 62. We spoke briefly through text and phone, but the canine senses kicked in, and I blocked every possible means of communication we had created. This was the easy part of the online process: I loved to write, so I often put on the charm in the form of poetry, and although I never smiled too much, I could take a decent picture for my profile. The scary part of the online dating scene was when you finally did find a good match, create conversation, and, yes, set up the first encounter with some strange woman you had only been conversing with for a couple of weeks.

With all that being said, I would check all the daily views I received from people interested, whether it be a smiley face, heart, or a brief message from one of the ladies, like, "Hi, how was your day?"

Being optimistic, I would always reply, being courteous and the gentleman caller. At this stage in my life, I wasn't looking for booty calls, just for some kind of friendship to engage in socially and take it from there and see how it went. Soon I found myself out on various dates anywhere from twenty minutes away from home to as far as two hours, but I was testing the waters. Believe it or not, if you remember the chapter on Maria, she was my 2-hour trek but well worth the company. Although this book touches on some extremely personal issues, I kept this short and highlighted my experience through a series of poems on how I felt when being with my new acquaintances.

LOLA

'Oh, dear Lord, she's been through so much in so little time. Make her well, feeling fine. Give her the strength, the will, the desire. Help her dig deep down and find the fire. She is still a mother of two yet so young, Dillion and Justin, her two sons. They are a family who shares so much; dear Lord, look over them with your gentle touch. I've seen her weak and strong, bringing back life before too long. She is a fighter who holds her own; she keeps things in check, running her home. I ask you to open the skies and look down upon them with restful eyes. Make her well; she's in need; take her hand, set her free. I see her smile oh so bright; the candle I hold, I now light. I will make a wish and say a prayer, oh dear Lord, sometimes life is not fair.'

Jasmine

'I just can't figure it out; her presence felt is what it's about. The two are cut from a different cloth, yet come together at no cost. The voice of reason she's brought to me; open my eyes, I now can see. Her existence is so serene; she brings much life with her eyes of green. Although she is so far from me, I feel her heartbeat inside me. Here I am, a bit naive, still living life heart on my sleeve. She has been through so much; help her heal with my gentle touch. I am a man with much emotion; I offer her genuine devotion. Thank you, Lord, you, hear my prayer; I now feel safe, no longer scared. Our lips have met, sending a vibe, a feeling I can't describe. She is a dream, however real; undescribed sex appeal.'

Morena

'I sit and view the winter frost; I must admit, in her absence, I am a bit lost; time passes, much a miss... So soft her gentle kiss. Dinner was prepared, and wine glasses were drawn. Where is she? Why am I waiting so long? Is it the job or maybe the child? While I am waiting, my emotions go wild. Is something wrong, or am I drawing conclusions? My mind playing tricks, creating illusions. If something were to happen, what to do? We just met, so who calls who? Although somewhat new to one another, our care and concern are stronger than the other. She is strong, inside and out. But when chaos wreaks havoc, often an unfair bout, My hand is held out for you to hold; I promise you never to grow cold. You don't have to look because you'll feel the presence. I am real; the time has come to rest your head, the strength needed to keep your life ahead; let me be your angel and hover above. You are one of God's creations for all to love.

Lisa

'There she sat at the bar; I stand so close, but yet still so far. I drove a distance taking time; now I sit sipping wine, the conversation overdue, time to share my voice with you. So much I'd like to share--the question is, will she care? Dig down deep, let it ride; be me; nothing to hide. I sit to her left and her to my right, quite a little twinkle in her eye; time to move this along, conversation flowing like a favorite song. Let's move away from this bar; the outside is not too far. A blank canvas we will paint. Will there be a next date? Do not rush; take your time. Enjoy her company; the sun will shine. Something's still much amiss when we will share our first kiss. We walk away hand-in-hand, nerves are gone, tall I stand. Looks like the day; much success; I think there will be a next.

Christi

'The time has come to share; don't be late. I'll meet you there. I'll hold the door and escort you through; so many questions on what to do. I start with a simple. How do you do? The ice has been broken, but the nerves are still there; if we want this to work, show each other we care. The dialogue is flowing forever clear; without question, you have my ear. It doesn't matter. My cards are in, so here we go... should I begin? I take a deep breath with a few small sighs, remembering to look into her eyes. Thank you for this opportunity.'

And of course, we can't always express the beauty we see in someone; but we can expose the false facade they portray:

Laura

'She's got a name, they call her danger, and a couple of drinks will sleep with any stranger. She'll make you a promise to your face, but deep down, an embarrassment to the human race. Says she's sick or at a wedding, only interested in her next bedding. Says she knows what she wants out of life; just be careful, she'll cut you like a knife. She posts her pics and I try not to stare; a great example of why life's unfair. Works from home and hates her boss, and not too long, that too will be lost. Kids are hungry; they need to eat, but mom's been drinking and can't stand on her own two feet. What a leader, so-called mother, barkeep, please pour me another. Tonight, is soccer, or is it dance? Or is it that guy in my pants? I don't know; it's just too much; another migraine just before lunch. Call a sitter; I need a fix; he'll come running, and I'll turn some tricks. In the meantime, send me a photo; I don't want to forget your name. That is a no-no. I don't know how she finds time to nap; a real employer wouldn't put up with that crap. They call it karma, and it's a bitch; when you're down can't climb out of that ditch. The days will come and go; there she'll sit all alone. Again, karma's a bitch, and her name is danger.'

CHAPTER 30: VESUVIUS ERUPTS AGAIN!!

Here we go again. Remember way back when I made a reference to having the Hershey squirts? (C-Diff infection). This time it'll be referred to more as having Mount Vesuvius erupt again. I couldn't figure out what was going on or what was worse. My diet was normal. I had no virus, but I continually needed to visit the restroom. No matter how often I went, I could not seem to relieve myself entirely. The feeling was so familiar; I didn't want to return to this unpleasant feeling, this uncertainty of when I would make my next trip to the bathroom, questioning if I could hold back or resist this powerful emission? If you also remember, in my earliest chapters, I had claimed using something to stimulate the same thing--a chocolatey substance. Something that tasted good and did its job (Exlax), allowing me to indulge in copious amounts of food. Well, I can tell you now the last thing I wanted to do was put one morsel of food in my stomach, for the fear it would only exit that much quicker. Now I looked to that chocolatey substance's alternate personality, which would do the opposite.

I looked at his friend Imodium. Hopefully, if I drank this stuff, I would stop for at least enough time to catch a break, give my butt cheeks a rest, and slow that constant cramping I could feel from the inside out that emerged each time I were to take a breath. Sometimes I just began drinking straight from the bottle, going through at least one bottle daily. Each time I went, I took another sip; ironically, this was not doing the trick. This went on for days. I started to miss work, lose sleep and weight, and even came to a point where I'd rather lie in my bed lifeless and let my bowels take over. They were out of control, letting things loose like a newborn when soiling their diaper, except the only one responsible for changing it would be me. In the past, I had experienced difficulties with my G.I. system, meaning my digestive system, where I constantly adjusted my diet and utilized various medications. Still, due diligence was never the end result. This time the doctors were right in the diagnosis (E-Coli) that the virus needed to continue its course until my system was free of this poisonous waste. The question now arose, where did I contract this un-intentional and un-forgiving cleanse? I prepared my meals, rarely dined out, and thoroughly washed produce.

Problems did not end there; the e-coli had wreaked internal and external havoc in my colon and anus area, forming fissures and razor-like cuts that burned like hell when sitting, passing gas, and engaging in a bowel movement. This went on for months, and despite any topical remedy being used, no relief or progress was being made in healing. Despite all the neuropathy and loss of sensation attributed to it, these tiny ulcer-like markings were superior in pain. If you have ever had a paper cut and then got lemon juice or vinegar in it after the fact, imagine that same experience between your butt cheeks at the exit of your colon. To kill the pain, creams like lidocaine and drugs like oxycodone were prescribed, yet the only result was the oxy would knock me out for a few hours in this whimsical land of nightmares. Even sith baths were suggested, which were basically soaking in a bath of warm water to dull the pain. It worked, the problem being only if I stayed submerged in the water.

Eventually, I would find there were times I would doze off while still in the tub; thankfully enough, I never drowned or swallowed too much water, but this treatment also ended when one evening, I found myself submerged in a pool of toxic waste. Obviously, my bowels would not wait for me to stop counting sheep and unleash their fury. I quickly pulled myself from the tub, feeling like Meryl Streep, playing the role of Karen Silkwood, where she was exposed to plutonium and being hosed down to rid the exposure, in this case, E Coli.

The following day, as if a detective, I needed to seek out the best in the business, a colon surgeon. At this point, the problem had far exceeded the specialties of a G.I. doctor. Long story short, this pain went on for months, as well as spasms within the pit of my stomach that seemed to come alive at night when trying to catch an hour's worth of sleep. A little research panned out in finding a surgeon at NYP whom I was familiar with, but again, she was not as close to home as I would have preferred. At least half the battle was completed because Dr. D had access to all my medical records and history; now, it was just being put through the physical exam. By this point in my life, I was ready to drop my drawers for any physician at the drop of a hat. I have been in this position so often that I have lost all my modesty.

There's no such thing as privacy anymore. I knew which way to bend, break, and twist... whatever was needed so the doctor could diagnose the situation. When she finally entered the room, I had already been laid on my stomach, legs spread, ready to rock. To make things a little more interesting, I started to whistle; I could only imagine the look on her face. She asked if I would like a gown or blanket to cover myself. I replied, "No, Dr. D., I'm good." At that point, I think I actually did hear a small snicker. As serious as the situation was, at least somebody could laugh, but on a more serious note, it had been confirmed that the situation needed to be addressed, and we would schedule surgery.

The surgery wasn't going to be anything major. It would be an outpatient procedure where Botox would be injected into my colon. First thing, I thought I knew what Botox was. I know it's normally used to generate or regain youth, to give you a better complexion or appearance. So why the hell were they injecting it inside of me? Botox works just as well in strengthening elasticity, much like facial skin, to strengthen your sphincter muscles within the colon. Whatever, I thought. As long as it works, I'll do it.

I was informed that the healing process would be 4 to 8 weeks, and some bleeding and incontinence would return for some time. Again being somewhat sarcastic yet humorous, I explained to the doctor that my modesty was gone. I'm all good now; I can purchase my own diapers. Can't wait to see what new designs they have.

To be honest, I think I had developed a defense mechanism where if I were concerned or a bit nervous about a certain situation in life-- in this case, surgery--I avoided the anxiety by not looking into the future and trying to mask it with sarcasm, still knowing there was some risk, but I was in good hands. I thought, "I've been battling conditions for 36+ years. In 4 to 8 weeks, I can do this standing on my head. Let's schedule this, get it done, and get some normalcy back in my everyday schedule."

The pain and discomfort continued, and I began to experience the return of the incontinence again. If you are old enough to remember the movie "History of the World-Part I," Mel Brooks tells one of the fair maidens, "Tickle your ass with a feather?" Her reply: "Oh yes, we are having some great weather." All I can say is the weather for me was like living in a monsoon, and all the complications just kept raining down on me. As for tickling my ass with a feather, if even something as subtle as a feather came near my ass right now, that would mean pain.

I did not have the luxury of waiting any longer and was prepped for colon surgery two days following my appointment with Dr. D. The procedure would be about two hours, which included the recovery phase, and the most intriguing part of this procedure was it would be done as an outpatient, assuming all went smoothly. I awoke to a very cheerful nurse who had done my vitals pre-surgery. She asked how I felt and said it would be okay to exit the hospital in another hour, seeing the effects of the anesthetic were still wearing off. I returned home, accompanied by my father, where I settled in my apartment. Dad ensured I was safe and asked if I needed anything before he left; I was good for now. About two weeks into recovery, it was happening again: the heavens were awakening, the chocolate factory was ready to re-open, and the volcano was returning to life. First, I thought the surgery wasn't successful or more optimistic, hopefully just the aftershocks of the surgery. Luckily, it was the second of the two, but on the other side, the downside was I was bringing back a sense of fashion I'd once worn--yup, diapers were back in style. This had gone on for several more weeks, and I will fess up that I thank God that diaper was strapped to my ass. Ultimately the side effects and any complications I was experiencing gradually subsided. I could go back to my Marky Mark CK boxer briefs, sometimes with a little reliance on a dose of the A.D. (Imodium) to curb any re-occurring problems. Still, despite all these complications, I knew I couldn't just throw in the towel. I wasn't ready to dig a ditch, jump in it, and pull the dirt over me, but this bullshit was not making it any easier to think that way.

"I am giving up on all my demons. Can't keep up with all their feelings. They string me along, and I don't belong. Out of sight, out of mind." - One OK R

CHAPTER 31: IRONY

I survived the many complications we experienced throughout this book and, unfortunately, still carry the burden of most of these issues, but I am alive. I try not to dwell on the past, where writing this book forced me to do so, but it acted much like a double-edged sword. On the one hand, to have to describe my mental and physical condition brought me to tears--I think more so for my family, who went through it with me, but it also became good tears and therapeutic. It is amazing when we tell ourselves that we cannot have total control over our future, but we definitely have enough to point it in the right direction. There is always something larger going on in one's life, and it's something called Fate. You see, I believe our stories, for the most part, are already written, and what was meant to happen probably will, but we may face obstacles in trying to reach those goals. I felt this chapter was important enough to share because I believe if you can train or coach your mind to think optimistically and positively, many of your attempted goals or achievements can be reached. True, when we use the word "goal," it is usually looking ahead at a gain or achievement, and I often stress not to get overly anxious about the future because of Fate. Still, I thought it necessary to share a piece I wrote when I was trained in life coaching. Now keep in mind I wrote this 20+ years ago:

'Christopher, today is another beautiful morning, a mirror of the success you have achieved. Your blood sugars are under control, and you exhibit endless energy with them. God is also with you, and together you will continue to educate and motivate others; their confidence in you inspires and fuels you.

For each and every person you mentor, you have made them aware of their purpose in life. With this accomplishment, you discover the experiences you create for others are infinite; you have become a mentor and realize your dreams are endless. Christopher, because you completed your Diabetes Education Training Program, you have gained great awareness of the importance of maintaining normal blood glucose levels for your continued success of a healthier you. You now find yourself enhanced with the knowledge gained from this course and contribute this knowledge to others, where their success has provided great reward. You have become a role model and mentor to others, and you exhibit your success by leading by example, showing just how energized you have become because you now have your blood sugars under complete control and find yourself exceeding your goals with diet and exercise. This success has an impact on your state of mind, allowing for such clear thoughts, everything about the control of your diabetes comes so naturally, and your confidence has grown stronger; the everyday task is a mere challenge that you take in stride, and you discover that what is experienced is handled much more easily than before.

With the confidence gained, you decide to generate awareness among others by branching out to other communities and increasing diabetes awareness through the support groups you have established to inspire others to see what you have accomplished. As a mentor, you provide wisdom, going beyond your original capabilities. The information you preach to others living with diabetes is now considered a tool for gaining strength and optimism in a healthier life. With this health, you become energized and realize there is a purpose; you have grown emotionally and financially. Your success and its impact have become so immense that people seek your advice, and with it comes financial prosperity. In fact, now that you are financially stable, you travel the world because you can. By doing so, your sense of well-being has increased, and you are free from everyday stress because you are now your own boss, and you realize you are in control of your future.

With this control and financial stability, you have opened a health and wellness center in your neighborhood, where you do not need to drive because it sits right behind the three family houses you now call home. The business is so successful because of the model of success you created for it, and it can practically run independently. This allows for more gained freedom and opportunity to explore.

You have no longer lonely in your travels, you have met your soulmate, and the possibilities are endless together. Through the grace of God, who you and your mate now realize is a mentor much like yourself, you have been blessed with two children, where your wealth exceeds the cost of raising a family in today's and even tomorrow's economy. You realize that your success has grown so much that college for the two has already been paid for, and your mate need not seek employment because there is no need. Much like your diabetes, you are in control, and the life you have provided for your family has provided some closure. You have become a mentor, husband, father, and role model, all emulated through the tools you provided to others in gaining endless success, where you have fulfilled each day in control with peace of mind.

Through your experience and success as a mentor, you continue creating awareness in people with diabetes. With your spiritual belief in God and the continued support of family and friends, you realize the message you have created is unlimited in the numbers you have guided toward health and wellness. You feel charged and ready to further this message through your well-being example. Your mind now works in harmony with your soul.

Reminder to listen daily.

The more and more you listen to this statement, the easier you realize how dreams are endless. As you listen to these words, instilled is the power and energy you have maintained to control your environment. By listening to the script daily, you are aware of how important you are to your family and community. The daily time allows for goals to become a reality and reality to become the world you control.'

Now for the would have, could have, and should have. Would I have followed my own motivational suggestion as a teen or adolescent? Probably not. Could I have listened to these, my own words, back then? No way, I was in denial, and no attempt at getting through to me would have worked. The obvious, though, is that I should have; where I do believe I probably would have experienced some of these complications to a lesser extent physically, but by practicing what I was preaching, I would have encouraged and provided self-help with my emotional stability, allowing me to live for the day, the present, and not dwell on the past, creating less concern or creation of un-needed anxiety over the future. Despite achieving many of my goals, there is still more room for growth. As a reference, I keep this statement folded up in my pocket, just in case I need a reminder not to look back at where I have come from but to see how far I have come.

SUMMARY

Although some may believe they are perfect, the fact is everyone susceptible to making a mistake is inevitable. However, we are all human. But this does present a choice. We can choose to overlook or ignore the error that was made or make the necessary changes preventing it from happening again. When we don't learn from our misfortune, we risk falling into a deeper hole. This buildup of unnecessary stress will not only affect you as an individual but also the others around you. As a result, you may lose their trust and your own self-understanding. I was lucky enough that despite not being able to comprehend my own behaviors, actions, and reactions, I was still embraced by my family, which is not always the case for some. At times I found myself unable to make ethical decisions creating a pattern of self-destruction.

After contemplating the publication of this book for many years, I found myself in need to share my story. Reliving the many medical situations I found myself in was difficult and therapeutic at the same time. I often found myself brought to tears, maybe more than the ink used to line the pages of this book.

I can only assume part of my hesitation was that I was still young and unwilling to share all the vulnerability, embarrassment, insecurities, fears, letdowns, and lack of promise I felt I should have achieved by this point. Now at 50 years old, I feel I have become wiser, increasing my awareness of life, and learned we only get one--fortunate for myself. I was given the opportunity and the chance at life more than once, much like a cat blessed with nine.

"In therapy, vulnerability gives the client the capacity to share their innermost thoughts, beliefs, and concerns openly. It provides them the opportunity to grow, heal and move on from their past" (Leroux et al., 2007). Jan 8, 2021

As a tool, poetry was a useful aid in helping me heal from the inside out. Poetry allowed me the space needed to be heard and understood. A safe place to go and unlock my emotion which was held back for so long. Through the words of poetry, this book is not meant to cure or to heal, and I cannot guarantee my methodology used will help you to become a better person or a healthier one or aid in curing whatever disease you suffer from. Despite all the misfortune that may be going on in your life, you need to find an outlet, encouraging a positive attitude and behaviors--one where you can escape, whether it be fifteen minutes, twenty minutes, an hour... whatever it takes to clear your mind and your soul, to heal from the inside-out; let's call it soul-searching.

Although controversial, the five stages of grief have been debated for some time, and some will argue that the stages do not occur chronologically, and some may not experience each one. In 1969, Elisabeth Kübler-Ross described five common stages of grief, popularly referred to as DABDA. They include:

- Denial

- Anger

- Bargaining

- Depression

- Acceptance

Regardless of the order, for most of my juvenile years through young adulthood, I visited each one, spending more time in some phases than others. Identifying most with Denial, Bargaining, and Depression. Looking back on my mental state at that period of time, I would have never been able to understand these stages. I wasn't programmed that way, and my focus was on instant gratification and not its consequences. I cannot say I coasted through these stages or reached total acceptance, but I have used stages like Denial to benefit my well-being and not hinder my progress. When you think life no longer makes sense and become overwhelmed by the littlest things, grief takes a backseat to Denial. Denial acts as a moderator. Stabilizing its progression, dulling its impact.

For the most part, anger will follow, and that's where poetry filled my void.

Although not much of a religious man, a lot of my poetry is an effort to reach out to a higher power and his army of angels. In doing so, my mind gradually slipped into the Bargaining phase. Offering my adherence to playing by the rules and making changes where needed. In trade, I rid my life of the many obstacles I've seen and avoid any in the future. Unfortunately, this is not always a deal that is signed and sealed or a mutual compromise. We are often left in question, "Does anyone hear what I am saying"? Having no answers to these problems leads to Depression.

You begin to alienate yourself, isolate yourself, and remove yourself from this picture. You create an inner sanctum much like the one I occupied. Leading to a downward spiral physically and mentally.

It's been years, and I can honestly say I have not completely met the acceptance of all my triggers in life. But it is a process. I have learned that we must be patient with progression and experience the good and the bad. Take what we've learned and move forward, making the necessary changes and embracing what proved productive in compliance with an acceptable position in life.

Realizing that not all days will be a good day, in turn, some bad. But these are not setbacks. Instead, lessons to learn from. When the bad days are overshadowed by the good, you have made progress and are ahead of the game.

First and foremost, you must be willing to make a change. Step up and accept the task of bettering yourself. Without you and your will, there is no catalyst. You must be the one to initiate the plan and follow through. Once you can do this, there is nothing wrong in reaching out to others, friends, family, Counseling, and possibly introducing prescribed medications:

"Push yourself because no one else will do it for you." – Anonymous.

I don't know the severity of the mental or physical state of the person who may choose to read this book, but I do know that at the time, my mind was not wired correctly, and I needed to find an outlet. It is more of a suggested method, in addition to whatever current treatment or care you are utilizing or even prescribed, and not meant to replace those necessities used to sustain life. Depending on who reads this book, from child to teen doctor or professional, I am sure I will get a mix of perspectives and opinions; but then again, that's what makes this world so diverse and challenging. Yes, I still live with many struggles, dealing with the physical and mental; however, through my process of poetic justice, I feel I have lessened the burden of these outside and internal pressures, alleviating a lot of stress in providing a more peaceful way of living one day at a time. I do honestly believe that if you have the desire, belief, and determination to move forward physically and mentally, you can do so. You have to be the one to make this choice, to want to better yourself, to help yourself in attaining emotional stability, and the strength to mentally push through these demands in what we call life. Many of the situations presented in the chapters of this book are not to emphasize how I struggled but to take these experiences, learn from them, and be able to comprehend or understand and make the connection with others in my shoes. My goal is not to look for sympathy but to stress empathy, providing comfort in knowing that there is somebody out there who truly understands this person and knows what goes into surviving the demand of existing in the world we live in today. One day at a time; this is enough. Don't look back and grieve over the past, for it's gone; don't be troubled about the future. Better yet, to come to live in the present and make it so beautiful that it will be worth remembering.

At this point in life, I have been through so many procedures that I have been given an expensive and thorough education provided by the top medical colleges and doctors; again, being considered the one percentile, I have experienced nothing that any scholastic institution has been able to replicate. I knew what would be commonly prescribed, but undoubtedly would not completely resolve my medical situation.

Despite the trials and tribulations diabetes presented, I still look at it as an educational experience, which I should've learned, listened to, and grown from it, regardless of the horrors. Looking back at one of the first chapters, I mention trophies, yet reaping no reward except the complication I still experience daily. Today I can say I did achieve a goal. I am still seeing the reward: an acknowledgment of being healthy enough to raise two exceptionally beautiful and talented children, not a tin trophy to put on a shelf, but having the opportunity to watch them grow, fulfill their dreams, and meet their milestones in something we call life. Live for today, for we do not know what tomorrow may bring.

ADDITIONAL POEMS: BY CHRISTOPHER

1) This is for the restless, not for the weak; for the voices,
I hear constantly speak. They tell me to do this and
not to do that, but viciously they return as a matter of
fact. I tried to listen; I tried to be fair. They'd come
back with much despair. I try not to listen; I try to be
fair. Ironically, they returned with not much care.
They push me this way, and over there, where I land,
they just don't care. They creep up and push me
around, in all positions, not unfamiliar ground. I try to
run, I try to flee, but soon they come to find me. It is
their being who start the brawl, making me feel two
inches tall. I don't have the power or much left in
pride, often thinking, try suicide. The time is come;
what shall I choose? No matter what I feel, it's like I'll
always lose. I need help. I need to fight; look to my
soul for some insight. My heart beats so ever fast; the
question is will it last? Hesitant to close my somber
eyes, scared to blink or compromise. He is not human,
just like you and me; slowly, he approaches choosing
my destiny. He will come when you're at peace, his
concern minimal, at the least. He approaches when no
others are around, turning your smile upside down.
He has taken my ability, the ability to walk, I try to
scream out but cannot talk. He's taking so much of
my will to fight and much of my pride from this
bastard I choose not to hide. I will pay back his favors
with revenge, my conscience stronger 'til the end. He
cannot beat me. Only choose to fight; I will survive
him, survive the night. He should just stop trying; he

should give in, see it is not I who creates sin. I look to the Lord. He gave me the prayer; now, the fight is much more fair. I have the strength, the will, and the desire; I will not burn in the devil's fire. Like the phoenix, I will rise high above, much like the peaceful white flying dove. A new lease on life I now begin, seeing the beauty that comes from within.

2) Send me an Angel. Let me hear her song. I have been praying for her much too long. Her whimsical words grace the air; however, this angel still cannot promise life to be fair. Continue to kneel. Continue to pray. I cannot promise another day. Live for today, not another, and enjoy the warmth of this peaceful summer. Mother Nature brings three more reasons: winter, spring, and fall are a few seasons. I cannot promise that I will come through, but there is much more for me to do. The sky lit bright red, and beautiful thoughts go through my head. I've been given a chance, another round, firmly placing my feet on the ground. With one step forward, I advance. Thank you, Lord, for the second chance. Where I'm headed, I don't know, but I walk a pace, a steady flow. Take a chance, look around; you'll never know where I might be found. Pass through my door, and you might see a new outlook on life and opportunity.

3) You see, it's my goal to show you peace; take my hand out I reach. Take my hand, feel my soul; let me show you my new role. I am not an angel but a man of peace; I practice what I preach. Turn to your heart, and listen from within; God shall forgive whatever sin. Take his gift of prayer; this is not any dare. With these words, create your story, pass it on, and restore the glory. Others may be out there waiting; show them love, and don't keep them hating. You feel the throb in your heart, despite it not being your job. You see, it is just part of life, so earn your wings, a small sacrifice. I sit quietly in my home, and suddenly, I feel alone. A tear trickles down my face. Is that salt I now taste? The temptation will present, and I am chosen, bringing fear, suddenly frozen. I don't know much about what to do, for now, I must look to you. My tears are much like the rain, the temptation so hard to refrain. I close my eyes and clench them tight, giving me the strength to endure this fight. You see, this is not round one or two; I've been here before; know what to do. This battle will drain me, so give me the strength; this fight has been so long in its length. I've taken many punches and gone down before picking myself up from the floor. I respond with a punch; hit or miss, the only thing guaranteed I'm tired of this. I have to choose to stay or go; my answer will be quick, not too slow. I've made my choice to continue to fight; I now close my eyes for a restful night.

4) You see, we all have angels. They come to us in different forms, one where's a cloak decked out in black, the other one present to fight off his attack. The one who wears black shows there's no hope and gets you prepared to tighten that rope. Cinched in tight, nowhere to go; one quick jerk, the result not slow. The other bears a dress of white and whispers in my ear I will help in this fight. She will come whenever I ask, fight the darkness rip off his mask. Although he now bears no disguise, his goal is to see salt drip from my eyes. He stays close and waits for me to vent, asking me Son do you consent. She hears the echo of my calling and realizes it's me slowly crawling. The battle to start surely begins; far from over, this competition is what lives within.

5) The days are long, and nights even longer; I cannot close my eyes, realizing I must be stronger. I have these goals that come from within, far from an angel where I have sinned. And most of my sins brought harm to me, unable to recognize I had a family. The journey for me forever growing, lack of patience in not knowing? For I am strong and willing to fight, will the future bring more wrong than right? This is a situation I have been before, the white light calling; for now, I slam that door.

6) Where did she go? Her picture is still here, no response; it's the rejection, I fear. I reach out to her not once but twice; a response to my hello would be quite nice. She shares her pictures, but I need more, a beautiful woman like never seen before. What grabs my attention I keep on file; for this girl, I'd drive the extra mile. She writes something brief and short, yet upfront, brutally honest, not just a stunt. When do I shut down? Call it a day; if I had the chance, so much I'd say. You see, I am a fighter; truth be told, it's a women's maturity and not how old. So, if I ever am blessed with this chance, without a question, I will ask her to dance. I'd take my time, for I am shy, but with no problem, look in her eye. Honest and open, I need her to feel my heart, strong as it beats, us never to part. Anyone can create a rhyme, but with poetry, a story takes some time. I must admit there is a communication providing much-needed motivation. You say you're looking for the ideal; just look across the room, for I am surreal.

MOTIVATIONAL QUOTES

"The greatest glory in living lies not in never falling, but in rising every time we fall." -Nelson Mandela.

"The way to get started is to quit talking and begin doing." -Walt Disney.

"Your time is limited, so don't waste it living someone else's life. Don't be trapped by dogma – which is living with the results of other people's thinking." - Steve Jobs

"If you look at what you have in life, you'll always have more. If you look at what you don't have in life, you'll never have enough." – Oprah Winfrey.

"When you reach the end of your rope, tie a knot in it and hang on." - Franklin D. Roosevelt.

"Always remember that you are absolutely unique. Just like everyone else." - Margaret Mead

"Don't judge each day by the harvest you reap but by the seeds that you plant." - Robert Louis Stevenson.

"The future belongs to those who believe in the beauty of their dreams." - Eleanor Roosevelt.

"It is during our darkest moments that we must focus on seeing the light." – Aristotle.

"You have brains in your head. You have feet in your shoes. You can steer yourself in any direction you choose." — Dr. Seuss.

Made in the USA
Middletown, DE
13 November 2023

42594787R00115